Praise for
Ready or Not: Leadership, Choices in Early Care and Education!

"Goffin and Washington have very succinctly captured and exposed our weaknesses. They have taken what many of us have been saying for years and framed it in a form of a blueprint for action. This call to action by Goffin and Washington is long overdue. They have very skillfully crafted their message for change and leadership in a passionate, yet scholarly, manner. There is something here for everyone; and to ignore the call would be tantamount to 'dereliction of duty.'"—**Josue Cruz, Jr.**, Bowling Green State University, Dean and Professor, College of Education and Administration, Past President NAEYC

"They get it! We need a true system of services for young children and their families in America. The authors explain to us why and present options for all of us to consider as we move forward."—**Dick Clifford**, Associate Director, National Center For Early Development, University of North Carolina at Chapel Hill

"The *Ready or Not* authors employ a variety of tactics to help us acknowledge imminent fork-in-the-road options in our field of early care and education. If not convinced by their analytical presentation, the collective voice of interview responses should make us embarrassed enough to take on the hard adaptive work they propose and prove to ourselves and others that we can tackle the challenges and make collective commitments about the future path for early care and education in our nation. If we fail to engage in this adaptive work we will be no better than our elected officials whom we criticize for their partisan stubbornness and refusal to collaborate for the good of the whole."—**Marilyn M. Smith**, Council for Professional Recognition, Washington, D.C.

"Whether you think the field of early care and education is at the tipping point or teetering on the edge, this book is unequivocally clear about one thing. Without courageous leadership from within, the destiny of what is now a wide array of child care and early education services will be in the hands of leadership from other service and industry sectors. In the most professional, constructive, and caring language possible, the authors build the case for setting a national agenda on strengthening the field through adaptive leadership. They show, through a finely crafted presentation of ideas, how turf and ideological conflicts are symptomatic of much more serious underlying problems that impede collective leadership. For those whose lives are enmeshed in the realities of the field, this book is on the mark and none too soon. Let's hope it's not too late."—**Karen Hill-Scott**, President, Karen Hill-Scott and Company, Culver City, California

"The frank and straightforward approach used in this book explicates the new realities and concerns for the field's future and contributes to the work involved in creating an early care and education system. In their examples, challenges, and strategies, Goffin and Washington also press readers to begin initiating critical self-examination and questioning such things as the tolerance for poor performance by colleagues, or the tendency to resist what the knowledge base of child development and early learning says is necessary for achieving good results for children. These are tough issues and challenges but *Ready or Not* includes guidance and resources such as an appendix with concrete examples of 'Early Care and Education's Changing Landscape' that will enable readers to create dialogue and discourse about the *new realities* in the field."—**Ed Greene**, Director, Educational Outreach and International Initiatives, Sesame Workshop, New York

"The authors pose wonderful questions and challenges for the field with their great insights. I love the way the book is laid out—GOOD job— and thanks!"—**Kathy Thornburg**, Director, Center for Family Policy and Research, University of Missouri

"Once I started reading, I could hardly put the book down. What a cogent and brilliant analysis the authors have put together!! The case is persuasive and soooo on-target. I admired the way the case was built, leading up to the hard (but accurate) assessment of the field; taking on the underlying issues of race and class was especially deftly handled. But I could say the same thing about many other aspects of this important book."—**Jane Henderson**, Policy Consultant and former Executive Director, First Five California

"'The king has no clothes on' . . . and it's time for all of us to seriously change our practice as early childhood educators. We must advocate for increased quality and professionalism from our field and not tolerate the poor quality of service we have delegated to families and children who arguably need the most resources. This book calls the question and that's my answer."—**Jason Sachs**, Director of Early Childhood, Boston Public Schools

EARLY CHILDHOOD EDUCATION SERIES
Leslie R. Williams, Editor

(continued)

Ready or Not

LEADERSHIP CHOICES IN EARLY CARE AND EDUCATION

Stacie G. Goffin and Valora Washington

Foreword by Marty Linsky and Ronald Heifetz

Teachers College, Columbia University
New York and London

Published by Teachers College Press, 1234 Amsterdam Avenue, New York, NY 10027

Library of Congress Cataloging-in-Publication Data

Goffin, Stacie G.
  Ready or not : leadership choices in early care and education / Stacie G. Goffin and Valora Washington ; foreword by Marty Linsky and Ronald Heifetz.
    p. cm. — (Early childhood education series)
  Includes bibliographical references and index.
  ISBN 978-0-8077-4793-3 (pbk : alk. paper) — ISBN 978-0-8077-4794-0 (cloth : alk. paper)
  1. Early childhood education—United States.   2. Educational change—United States.   3. Educational leadership—United States.   I. Washington, Valora, 1953– II. Title.

  LB1139.25.G64 2007
  372.21—dc22   2007003919

ISBN 978-0-8077-4793-3 (paper)
ISBN 978-0-8077-4794-0 (cloth)

Printed on acid-free paper
Manufactured in the United States of America

14 13 12 11 10 09 08   8 7 6 5 4

Contents

Foreword

The book you are about to read offers a powerful and compelling leadership challenge to the good and noble people who work in early care and education. It is also in itself an act of leadership.

As teachers, authors, and consultants on leadership, we have come to believe that leadership is best understood not as a person, or a package of characteristics or traits, but as an activity, a set of behaviors that can be undertaken by anyone independent of position. Leadership is not the prerogative of those who aim or succeed in getting a big job. Leadership is open to anyone who has the courage and skill to try to mobilize people to address their most difficult issues, what we call their Adaptive Challenges.

Because it is dangerous and difficult, the exercise of leadership often comes from people who are not in positions of authority, and not only notables like Gandhi, Mother Theresa, Martin Luther King Jr., and Nelson Mandela, but also a myriad of courageous unsung everyday initiators whose names we do not know because articles and histories are not written about them. People in big jobs have too much at stake personally to risk stepping into leadership's turbulent terrain.

So it is not surprising that this courageous wake-up call to those working in early child care and education should come from two women who know the field intimately from a half-century of collective years of service and experience, but do not presently hold positions of formal authority.

The authors, Stacie Goffin and Valora Washington have asked us to write this foreword because they have used the frameworks and ideas we have developed and use in our work, called Adaptive Leadership, in observing, interpreting, and intervening in the current reality in early care and education.

Those three steps—Observation, Interpretation, and Intervention—are three key behaviors for leadership.

Goffin and Washington have done their work well. First, they have taken a distanced view of the field—a View from the Balcony, in our language. They have collected data from various sources, including their own research, and brought it all together to create an unemotional snapshot of the current reality. That's the Observation part. Then they have created meaning from the factual snapshot by making an Interpretation of what they found, an interpretation that is likely to disturb many of those in and around the field because it holds them accountable for their role in the current crisis of purpose, identity, and responsibility in the field as well as for the solution to it. Finally, they have written this book, made an Intervention, based on their interpretation, carefully tailored to maximize the chances of success. The intervention itself is artful from a leadership perspective. They have taken several steps to give their ideas the best possible chance at being taken up: They have acknowledged the wonderful work that has happened to date in the field; they have framed the adaptive issues that need to be addressed; they have used a medium and a style that will be accessible to all the stakeholders; and they have tried to avoid making themselves the issue by stopping short of taking a position on what the outcomes ought to be.

Nevertheless, as the authors acknowledge, even posing the issues as they do will be experienced as threatening by many of those now in the field. That's what makes Adaptive Leadership dangerous. By asking questions no one wants asked, people exercising adaptive leadership generate pushback. Resistance will surely come here as well, although we expect it will take many forms, passive and active. Our guess is that the most powerful form of resistance will be to try to ignore the challenge because those in the early care and education system have accommodated to the status quo, made it work for them. Entertaining the Goffin-Washington challenges in a serious way will feel risky to anyone who has an investment in the way things are and will see the possibility of losing something important if the performance gap and credibility gap that the authors identify are seriously addressed.

But adaptation, and the process of doing adaptive work, is as much about conservation and preservation as it is about loss. The hard work that Goffin and Washington have challenged the field to do is to have the will to identify what of all that they have accomplished, what of all that has gotten the field to where it is today, what of all the values and loyalties that are currently honored, is so much of the essence, the core of the field's DNA, that it needs to be preserved going forward. And then, what is the 10% or 20% of the current DNA that is expendable, and must be left behind in order to go forward and thrive in a new reality.

If you are reading this, you are probably a person committed to early care and education. If so, you have the luxury of finding meaning and purpose in your life every day without having to search for it. There is no more noble calling. For us, this book helps us do the same. That some of the ideas we have been working on, refining, and disseminating for a quarter of century might be useful to a field of work that is so important to the future of the planet gives our lives meaning and purpose as well.

Marty Linsky and Ronald Heifetz
Co-founders of Cambridge Leadership Associates
and longtime faculty colleagues at Harvard's
John F. Kennedy School of Government

Acknowledgments

We are indebted to the many people whose contributions made this book better.

At the top of the list are members of our Advisory Group. This extraordinary group of individuals brought a great deal of wisdom and expertise to this project. We are grateful for their willingness to give of their time in reading drafts of our work and sharing their insights with us. Advisory Group members were as follows:

Charles Bruner, Executive Director, Child and Family Policy Center, Iowa

Harriet Dichter, Deputy Secretary, Office of Child Development, Early Learning, Pennsylvania Department of Education and Public Welfare

Stephanie Fanjul, President, North Carolina Partnership for Children

Peg Sprague, Vice President, United Way of Massachusetts Bay, Boston

Caroline Zinsser, Retired Program Officer, Rockefeller Brothers Fund

Funding from the Foundation for Child Development (FCD) supported our work in numerous ways: by enabling us to conduct interviews with the field's key leaders; by supporting focus groups; by hosting a meeting of our Advisory Group; and by allowing us to travel to various venues to refine and extend our work. Special thanks go to Fasaha Traylor, Program Officer at FCD, for her guidance and assistance.

Special thanks also are due to Marie Ellen Larcada and Susan Liddicoat, our editors at Teachers College Press. Donna Smerlas, Sophia Bishop-Rice, and Heather Fox provided administrative assistance. We acknowledge these three individuals with gratitude, as well as Lesley University, which managed our grant from FCD.

Throughout this work, we had the good fortune to present our ideas at several conferences. The National Association for the Education of Young Children (NAEYC) offered presentation opportunities at its 2005 and 2006 annual meetings and the 2006 Professional Development Institute, as did the McCormick Tribune Center for Early Childhood Leadership at its 2006 annual conference. Participants in these sessions contributed in important ways to our thinking.

We are especially grateful that so many exceptional people agreed to share their ideas with us in personal interviews and focus groups. We asked probing questions, and no one refused to openly reveal their frustrations and aspirations for the field. In order to protect the confidentiality that we offered as a condition for open and forthright discussion, we intentionally do not attribute comments in the book to named individuals.

Throughout the book, we frequently refer to what we learned from these conversations and accept responsibility for how we have interpreted the interviewees' ideas. Gratefully, these individuals, whose names are listed below, gave us permission to identify their involvement with our work and to share what we learned from them.

Finally, we are indebted to our families, who have wholly embraced us during the time of this work. Stacie's husband, Bruce, sustained us with wonderful meals and stimulating conversation. Valora's mother, Elizabeth Barbour, provided "teen care" for daughter Kamilah during absences from home; adult son Omari happily accepted chauffeur and chaperone duties for the busy teen. We realize how lucky we are to have such incredibly supportive loved ones.

PARTICIPANTS IN INDIVIDUAL INTERVIEWS

J.D. Andrews	Sarah Greene
Steve Barnett	Karen Hill Scott
Barbara Bowman	Sharon Lynn Kagan
Sue Bredekamp	Lilian Katz
Charles Bruner	David Lawrence
Richard Clifford	Michael Levine
Josué Cruz	Joan Lombardi
Jerlean Daniel	Luba Lynch
Harriet Dichter	Linda Mason
Libby Doggett	Anne Mitchell
Stephanie Fanjul	Kathy Modigliani
Ellen Galinsky	Gwen Morgan
Danielle Gonzales	Dori Mornan

Don Owens
Jolie Bain Pillsbury
Cheryl Polk
Sue Russell
Magali Sarfatti-Larson
Marilyn Smith
Louise Derman Sparks

Phil Sparks
Peg Sprague
Lauren Tozi
Fasaha Traylor
Susan Uhran
Marcy Whitebook
Marci Young

FOCUS GROUP PARTICIPANTS

Doug Baird
Carol Brunson Day
Libby Doggett
Stephanie Fanjul
Barbara Kamara
Dorie Mornan
Gwen Morgan

Wanda Newell
Teresa Perry
Jeri Robinson
Elizabeth Schaefer
Peg Sprague
Maurice Sykes
Yasmina Vinci

STRUCTURED INTERACTIONS

We are also grateful to the approximately 250 "anonymous" people who participated in sessions we presented at NAEYC's annual conferences and Professional Development Institute, and at Leadership Connections, sponsored by the McCormick Tribune Center for Early Childhood Leadership.

Introduction

It is time to call the question: *What defines and bounds early care and education as a field?*

During more than 50 years of collective experience in early care and education, we have had multiple opportunities to work as change agents at the local, state, and national levels. As college teachers and administrators, foundation and not-for-profit executives, and independent consultants, we have deeply lived the field's evolution from a relatively invisible enterprise to a field on the cusp of being recognized as providing a public good.

During the lifespan of our careers, we have witnessed enormous growth in the number of programs and personnel in the field and the number of organizations that engage with this work. A mostly obscure occupation when we entered college as undergraduates, the knowledge base on the care and education of young children has exploded. Working with polling, financial, and marketing experts, the field's leaders have succeeded in widely disseminating the findings: "the early years are learning years"™ and can change the life trajectories of poor children and fuel economic growth.[1]

As a result, the early care and education field has burgeoned into a large—albeit fragmented—enterprise. It now has measurable impact on states' and the nation's economic vitality. Advocates have successfully increased state investments in early care and education. Policy makers and business leaders have embraced our work and made it part of a national dialogue.

This would seem to be the best of times.

But if so, why do we—and the hundreds of people to whom we have spoken or listened in interviews, focus groups, and structured interactions —feel so anxious about the field's future?

We think at least two reasons exist for this anxiety: For one, the gulf is widening between promises made and promises realized. Although many states have great expectations for their emerging prekindergarten programs, few have aligned their public investments with the program elements outlined by program evaluations as the basis for promising child outcomes. Despite growing public acceptance of children's school readiness as a rationale for investing in early care and education, few states— or the federal government—are aligning their rhetoric with what is known about children's early learning. Over time, this misalignment could set the stage for the public's disillusionment with early care and education as an important contributor to children's, and society's, well-being.

Second—and in our minds, even more significant in terms of more immediate consequences—is the early care and education field's lack of clarity about its purpose, identity, and responsibility. Despite its many accomplishments, the field largely has been unwilling or unable to develop a coherent definition of itself and its work. It cannot even agree on a name— is it, for example, early care and education or early education and care?— and the differing viewpoints on these and other issues evoke passionate debate.

With high teacher and administrator turnover rates and with declining college preparation levels for individuals entering the field as teachers, most staff working in direct services have neither the knowledge base nor the socialization needed to achieve the child outcomes touted in landmark evaluation studies. There is deep-seated division—even resentment and hostility—about issues such as occupational qualifications and the intersection of race and class with accountability for child and program results. Further, we have yet to speak to a group of people who can agree on the core focus, intentions, or expected outcomes of the field's work.

For those individuals outside of early care and education who seek our input and guidance, the field's lack of clarity and cohesion about its work produces confusion and frustration. As a result, these leaders often choose to move their early care and education agendas without us, minimizing the field's influence in advancing itself and its work.

For all of these reasons, anxiety and uncertainty about the future permeate the field.

WHY WE WROTE THIS BOOK

We, as authors, believe that early care and education is in the midst of a historical shift: from being relatively unknown to being highly visible, and from concentrating on new program development and expansion to building a system of programs and services capable of providing consistently high-quality results. This is a significant time for early care and education, and it is a defining moment for the field's future. Yet, no rush of activity, slogans, or rallying cries can mask the fact that the field itself is on a treadmill, not a pathway.

If those of us in early care and education want to be more than just observers of this moment in the field's evolution, we need to establish a firm foundation for the field's future and its value as a specialized field of endeavor. Thus, we need to resolve how the field of early care and education is defined and what delineates its boundaries. Having a central role in shaping the field's future is contingent on our being able to provide an answer to this seminal field-defining issue. That is why, as authors, drawing on terminology from parliamentary procedures, we believe it is time to "call the question." The field's indecision has gone on far too long.

This book makes a case for the field's need to face up to its new realities and to confront the choices these new realities thrust upon it. We want this book to provoke the field-wide self-analysis and decision making that are necessary for breaking through decades-old deadlocks, catalyzing significant change, and creating the adaptability needed to thrive in a complex, competitive, and challenging environment. The ability to find consensual answers to questions about purpose, identity, and responsibility will determine the field's ability to go forward with a clear articulation of its collective competence and responsibility to children and families.

There are no preexisting answers for the field-defining questions we are posing. As a result, we frame the field's issues as adaptive challenges and advocate for the potential of adaptive work to support the field's decision making and build future leadership capacity. To our knowledge, we are among the first to suggest that adaptive leadership, as conceptualized by Ron Heifetz,[2] can be used with an occupational field of endeavor.

Our advocacy in this regard comes from a basic premise of adaptive leadership work: Answers for the critical issues faced by the field reside within those of us who own the adaptive challenge. If we are to assume a greater leadership role on behalf of early care and education as a public good, and for the system that delivers it, we cannot rely on others to resolve our issues. Thus this leadership work needs to be our work.

It will not be easy, however. Our adaptive work will likely evoke difficult debate, painful decisions and choices, and the loss of some of the field's historically cherished positions. Additionally, because of the nature of adaptive work, we will not be able to rely on the wisdom of a few leaders from the field. Resolving the field's adaptive challenges, especially in the context of its new realities, necessitates moving beyond reliance on individual leaders and toward creation of a field-wide community of diverse leaders.[3]

From interviews, focus groups, and structured interactions with leaders in the field, it is clear to us that our point of view has struck a receptive chord. People eagerly engage with the field-defining questions that we have identified and with the need for doing this work.

DEFINING OUR TERMS

At this point, it seems important to define the terms that we use throughout this book. By *early care and education*, we mean those programs that directly seek to support and enhance children's early development and learning, regardless of a program's auspices. We view the *early childhood field* as an inclusive term that encompasses early care and education, as well as the complementary work performed by colleagues in physical and mental health and social services.[4]

We consider the phrase *early care and education* to be imprecise, however, and use it primarily because of its wide acceptance. The phrase was coined in the 1990s to overcome the field's fissure between its "care" and "education" sectors and to promote to the general public the inseparability, from a child's perspective, of care and education.[5] At the time, many of us viewed this unifying phrase as a transitional term. We still do, and suspect that its continued use reflects the field's ambiguity regarding its primary purpose.

Finally, for the meaning of *field* we rely on Margaret Wheatley's definition: an invisible world filled with mediums of connections, an invisible structure that connects.[6] Wheatley's definition offers a flexible framework for contemplating what bounds us as a field and permits us to bypass definitional and other issues associated with the term *profession*.[7]

HOW THE BOOK IS ORGANIZED

We envision this book as a leadership manifesto. In Chapter 1 we begin by making a case for the field's uncertain future and present six field-defining questions. Chapter 2 follows with a presentation of new realities that have fundamentally altered the context for the field's present and future leadership work. These new realities significantly influence the decision-making options available in responding to the six field-defining questions.

Chapter 3 then presents the "necessary choices" that the field must confront in order to bring clarity and coherence to the three overarching issues of purpose, identity, and responsibility. This chapter also identifies decision elements associated with each of the six field-defining questions.

Chapter 4 concludes the book by describing adaptive work in greater detail and underscores the importance of responding to the field's adaptive challenges through a field-wide and inclusive process. Our intent is to spur the leadership work necessary for making consensual decisions about the six field-defining questions and, ultimately, for answering the question of what defines and bounds early care and education as a field.

CALLING THE QUESTION AS A MATTER OF INTEGRITY

Despite the rhetoric and expressed convictions, field-based research and experience make abundantly clear that all too often:

- Those of us in the field resist doing what our knowledge base says is necessary for achieving good results for children.
- We are willing to tolerate poor performance by our colleagues.
- We hesitate to improve ourselves and our programs if doing so involves too much effort or cost.
- We postpone change and thus defer its benefits to future generations.

This book seeks to address the disparity between the field's convictions and its behavior, which by definition indicates an adaptive leadership challenge. We acknowledge the many issues confronting early care and education. Yet addressing this disparity is essential if the early care and education field is to have *integrity*, defined by Carter as "the courage of our convictions [and] the willingness to speak and act in behalf of what we know is right."[8]

This is *our* work. Without it, the field's integrity is at stake. With it, the field's adaptive challenges offer an exciting and timely opportunity to engage with one another to move the field forward on behalf of children.

CHAPTER 1

Calling the Question

The history of early care and education is marked by numerous accomplishments. Beginning in the mid-19th century, programmatic accomplishments include the spread and institutionalization of kindergarten, preschool, Head Start, and child care.[1] The most recent foray into program development is the effort to reform preschools and establish prekindergarten for 4-year-olds as part of the nation's K–12 education system.[2] Collectively, these programs and their histories have fashioned the early care and education field's present occupational identity and forged allegiances to discrete programs.

As the 20th century drew to a close, early care and education leaders began shifting their focus and directing attention to conceptualizing and building the professional, financial, and governance structures needed to sustain program quality over time. This systemic focus, which began in the early 1990s, emerged from escalating demand for early care and education services, early childhood education's growing visibility, and the need to bring improved quality and coordination to an increasingly fragmented and disorganized array of programs and services.

Almost 2 decades later, in the first decade of the 21st century, a majority of states are engaged with early care and education system-building efforts.[3] Now, the prospect of a coherent early care and education system increasingly serves as a filter for assessing the advent of new programs and policies.[4] Commenting on the trend toward universal pre-kindergarten, for example, Morgan and Helburn noted, "Universal Pre-K as a trend is too new to determine whether it can be incorporated into a seamless mixed delivery system of auspices, or just one more competing 'program' adding to the problems in the system."[5]

BUILDING AN EARLY CARE AND EDUCATION SYSTEM

Thus, the field's focus is veering from new program development to system building, with the intent of bringing coherence, sustainability, and consistently higher performance to a field that to this point has lacked all three. Yet, moving from an array of loosely coupled programs to a coherent early care and education system has been challenging.

We recognize that the term *systems* might be more accurate given that system development is occurring primarily at the state level; still, we intentionally are focusing on what unites, rather than what differentiates, system development in early care and education. System development requires going beyond the theoretical and philosophical debates about curriculum and pedagogy that for so long have dominated the interests of the field's leaders.[6] It requires knowledge of a system's parts and interrelationships and, among other things, specifics about financing, agreement about what early educators need to know and be able to do, decisions about how the system should be governed, and unity on the outcomes for which the system, in general, and programs, in particular, should be responsible. It demands focusing on what should be common to all early care and education programs and on accountability for results.

Kagan and Cohen define an *early care and education system* as programs plus infrastructure.[7] While the early care and education system elements are largely known,[8] still in question is how this evolution will play itself out. A primary contributor to this mystery is the future scope and role of the early care and education field itself.

Efforts to build an early care and education system have made apparent the field's lack of consensus about its work and the disagreements that characterize attempts to find common ground. As a result, the structure and design of a future early care and education system—and whether it will emerge as a single system—are unclear. Also unknown is the extent to which, as a field, we will significantly inform and influence the decision making involved with this work.

OUR POINT OF VIEW

The concept of early care and education as a public good and as an integral part of our national infrastructure appears to be approaching a threshold of acceptance.[9] Policy makers and others who historically have expressed little interest in our field have begun driving the formative system-building efforts that are underway in many states.

Yet becoming fully accepted as a public good and integrated into the national infrastructure will require our being able to organize the field so it can fulfill the public's emerging mandate. The actual work of implementing system change will require our being able to exercise effective political leadership.

Thus, when thinking about the field's leadership needs, we need to extend beyond a focus on individual leaders—beyond conversations about administrative leadership,[10] breakthroughs in defining the domains and functions of individual leadership,[11] and efforts to define pathways for developing individual leadership expertise.[12] To affect political decision making and exert influence during moments of opportunity, field-wide leadership is needed—leadership that can act with a coordinated voice on behalf of young children and their early care and education. *To achieve this end, though, field-wide leadership must be able to represent a coherent field of practice.* Given the early care and education field's current state of affairs, however, creating a coherent field of practice is unlikely unless we confront what, in fact, it means to be a *field* for early care and education.

Early care and education is increasingly the focus of federal, state, and local policy discussions, of business roundtables, and of economic analyses.[13] New policy and administrative decisions routinely are being implemented, with varying levels of consultation with early care and education leaders. As expressed by one of our interviewees, "The field is being led rather than leading."

Others' reluctance to consult with us can be attributed to several factors: the field's indecision about its responsibilities; too often appearing to resist change indiscriminately; routinely focusing on sector differences rather than on creating common ground; and avoiding difficult issues and decisions.

We would contend, however, that even if the field were extensively consulted, the results would be uneven—because the field lacks a consistent and unambiguous point of view about the purpose of its work and about what defines its shared identity and responsibility. As a result, the early care and education field lacks a shared "sense of purpose, possibility, and mutual commitment."[14] Our individual interviews with 40 of the field's state and national leaders affirm this perception.[15]

For all these reasons, we believe it is time to call the question: What defines and bounds early care and education as a field?[16]

Calling the Question

We recognize that risk may be involved in "calling the question." Our use of straightforward language may be perceived as unnecessarily provocative. Providing an "insiders' view" may raise concerns that we are placing important work at risk. To some, we may come across as overly critical or underappreciative of work currently in process. Still others may personalize our comments and take offense. While realizing that all of these responses are possible, none of them match our intent or capture our deep commitment to the field.

Still, based on participation in numerous change initiatives and extended conversations with participants in others, we question whether an almost exclusive focus on the external conditions impeding the field's success will increase the consistent availability of quality early learning experiences. In fact, it feels irresponsible to us that the field has yet to "own up" to the ways in which its actions (and, as often, inactions) contribute to the incoherence of its delivery system and the uneven quality of early care and education programs.

We are not the first to call the question of what binds early care and education as a field. In 1967, in the midst of heated debates about the most effective early childhood education program models, researcher and activist Bettye Caldwell noted, "While a great deal of attention is currently being given to fostering concept formation in young children, there appears to be relatively little concern with concept formation *about* the field most intimately concerned with child development." Why can we not, she asked, be more explicit about our goals and objectives?[17]

Twenty years later, in marking the 60th anniversary of NAEYC, executive director Marilyn Smith described three challenges needing to be overcome to achieve visions for the year 2000. She labeled the third and most difficult challenge as follows: "We MUST unify the field of early childhood education." She then went on to say, "The greatest obstacle, and yet the one that could have the most positive impact on services to children and their families, is to find ways to negate the dichotomies that split our field apart. There are many 'us' versus 'them' divisions in the early childhood field."[18] Her list of divisions is amazingly contemporary; 20 years later, we navigate and argue over many of these very same dichotomies:

- Academicians versus practitioners
- Profit versus not-for-profit programs
- Preschool versus child care
- Educational program goals versus social program goals
- Black versus White/Hispanic or Asian versus Native American
- Preschools versus elementary schools

Responding to the Question

The 1960s and 1980s, the timing for Caldwell's and Smith's comments, were times of upheaval for early care and education. Now, in the first decade of the 2000s, the field is once again in a time of extensive change—change that will have profound implications for early care and education, the early care and education field, and the children, families, and society being served.

As authors, we have concluded that moving forward depends on engaging in a process of deep and honest examination and appraisal of beliefs, assumptions, and past actions—with the intent of creating a common platform for defining early care and education and describing the field that delivers its programs and services. A field-level response to the central question of definition and boundaries is prerequisite to providing a viable foundation for effective leadership and developing an early care and education system. Further, without field-wide leadership, early care and education will be stymied continually by the lack of a collective voice.

In the absence of collective self-examination and a willingness to "distinguish those norms and values worth preserving from those that have become antiquated and dysfunctional,"[19] early care and education leaders will continue to be placed in a position of responding to others' leadership rather than being active and influential partners in the future being formed.

While this is a time filled with ambiguity because of political and economic uncertainties, new external demands, and the entry of decision makers unfamiliar with the complexities of our field, it also is a time filled with exciting possibility. If we in the field choose, we can use this fluidity and growing interest in our work to take greater charge of the field's future and the future we want for children.

THE LEADERSHIP WORK OF THE EARLY CARE AND EDUCATION FIELD

The leadership required by the field at this point in time transcends the "dauntless women,"[20] men, and associations that so ably led the field when its focus was on program development and expansion. Needed now is a networked, field-wide leadership capable of envisioning, advancing, and executing complex systemic change.

In expressing the motivation for their important 1997 book, *Leadership in Early Care and Education*, Kagan and Bowman wrote that they were "inspired by the conviction that greater attention needs to be given to the development and support of leaders *in the field* of early care and education."[21] By way of contrast, we are motivated by the need to build coherent leadership *for the field*—field-wide leadership built from a shared foundation and generated through coordinated networks of individual and institutional leadership at local, state, and national levels.

Strong field-wide leadership is needed to bolster the field's political capacity to significantly sway public decisions about early care and education and to effect durable change within the field. It is needed to enhance the ability to influence how local, state, and federal levels of government work together to fund, regulate, and support early care and education services and, in turn, to ensure coordination with related systems essential to children's overall healthy development. Yet these outcomes cannot be achieved in the absence of clarity regarding answers to the question of what defines and bounds early care and education as a field.

Taking Responsibility

If we want to create a shared platform for early care and education, the field must take responsibility for the collective problem solving the construction will require. All of us have to do the hard work of collective adaptation—of making decisions and choices about the 21st-century characteristics of the early care and education field. It is the need for sustained and focused self-examination—in order to create a consensual answer to the question of what defines and sets the boundaries for the early care and education field—that makes relevant the work of Ron Heifetz and his colleagues on adaptive leadership.[22]

Heifetz makes a distinction between technical problems and adaptive challenges. Technical problems involve the application of existing knowledge and expertise to problems. The availability of accepted answers to a problem makes it possible to focus on finding and applying known solutions.

In contrast, when the challenges require adaptive leadership, preexisting solutions do not exist for identified problems. Rather, those of us attempting to resolve the challenges must engage in the work of developing acceptable solutions and of making the required adaptations. Adaptive work often demands developing new values, habits, and behaviors. It is made harder by the fact that outside parties cannot do this work for us *because it is the field's existing habits, attitudes, and behaviors that are contributing to the issues that must be confronted.*

Addressing Field-Defining Questions

Adaptive work is about change—about changing how the field approaches its work, our relationship with one another, and our relationship with others external to the field. Adaptive work is characterized by conflicting values and/or the presence of gaps between the values people stand for and the reality they face. Adaptive work strives to close the distance between people's espoused values and their actual behaviors, work that by its nature usually necessitates painful trade-offs.[23]

Earlier, we posed as a central uncertainty, "What defines and bounds early care and education as a field?" This uncertainty emerges from what we believe to be the field's two adaptive challenges:

1. A *performance gap* that calls for closing the distance between an expressed commitment to children's high-quality early care and education and the field's uneven collective competence
2. A *credibility gap* that calls for closing the distance between the desire to be recognized as leaders on behalf of early care and education and the field's self-protective behaviors

Known answers for addressing these gaps do not exist. We believe that finding these answers should become central to the field's leadership work. By way of assistance, we offer six field-defining questions as a scaffold for the leadership work we are advocating.

Three defining issues organize these six field-defining questions: purpose, identity, and responsibility. Deliberating the six field-defining questions, and the decisions and choices they require, can help ascertain what defines and bounds the work of this collective enterprise. Finding consensual answers can determine whether the early care and education field is justified in identifying its work as a specialized and accountable field of endeavor and competence.

PURPOSE

1. What is the early care and education field's defining intent?
2. Does the field's intent vary by setting or by auspice (e.g., centers and schools; regulated family child care; license-exempt family, friend, and neighbor care)?
3. What chronological span describes the ages of children served (e.g., birth to the start of kindergarten; birth through kindergarten; birth to age 8; prekindergarten through grade 3)?

IDENTITY

4. What is the field's distinctive contribution and competence as a collective entity?[24]
5. Is early care and education a single/unified field of endeavor or a field comprising subfields (such as health care, for example)?

RESPONSIBILITY

6. To what extent are we, as a field, willing to hold ourselves accountable to one another and to be held publicly accountable for results in return for the autonomy to deliver programming based on the field's knowledge base?

The current unavailability of consistent answers to these six field-defining questions presents a barrier to system design efforts and to the delivery of consistently high-quality early care and education. The fact that the field does not even agree on a name for its work[25]—early care and education, early education and care, early childhood education, early education and child care, early care and learning, educare, early learning, early education—provides concrete evidence of role confusion and public evidence of internal divisions. The field's willingness to advocate that others should respond to children's needs and potential based on what is known, without holding itself similarly responsible for acting on this knowledge, reveals its hesitation to be held accountable for what it does. The frequency and angst with which the field questions who is deciding the future of early care and education exposes anxieties and fears about shared leadership.

As a result, individuals outside of the field often step forward to create the answers. As noted a decade ago by Kagan and Bowman, "Finally, and most fundamentally, leadership in early care and education cannot be defined until the field defines what constitutes early care and education."[26]

Recognizing That Change Is Not Optional

Ultimately, our sense of urgency as authors about the need for responding to the leadership challenge of articulating what defines and bounds the early care and education field comes from the following:

- Despite the dedicated efforts of early care and education leaders, far too many children are in early care and education programs of mediocre quality.[27]
- Too few policy makers fully understand the barriers that must be bridged if this empirical fact is to be changed.
- Far too few practitioners are prepared for their responsibilities.[28]

At the same time, knowledge about the importance of childhood development and about children's learning capacities has become more robust, refined, and available to the public.[29] As a result, public expectations have risen regarding the educational contributions of early childhood education, accompanied by increased public and private investments.

The new realities described in Chapter 2 make evident that as a field we no longer can afford to be bystanders. The early care and education field is being redefined. The fact of this transformation no longer is in question. Rather, the question is the extent to which early educators will have the opportunity to be part of—and influential in—this crucial work.

If as a field we rebuff the challenge of deliberating and responding to the defining choices around purpose, identity, and responsibility, others will feel empowered to make these decisions for us. If as a field we avoid responsibility for doing adaptive work, we limit our present and future capacity to lead on behalf of early care and education. By failing to mobilize ourselves to do this leadership work at this time, we reduce our chances to shape the early care and education field so it can most benefit young children, and we lessen our prospects for being recognized as legitimate spokespersons for the focus and design of an early care and education system.

PREVIOUS ADAPTIVE WORK IN EARLY CARE AND EDUCATION

As we undertake our adaptive work, we can look to the history of the early care and education field for earlier examples. The first and most powerful example extended from 1903 through 1913. Led by the Committee of Nineteen under the sponsorship of the International Kindergarten Union, the 10-year debate sought to "formulate contemporary kindergarten thought."[30] The results led to the embrace of developmentally appropriate practice as the field's defining pedagogy, which, in turn, has formed the symbolic core of our shared identity.

The impetus for the adaptive work by the Committee of Nineteen is noteworthy for its parallels to our own circumstance. According to Synder's summary of this transformative time:

> Not only was the world the new [early childhood] leaders faced very different and far more complicated than that in which the early leaders had worked, but the challenge within education itself was very different. . . . The new leaders . . . were confronted with the problem of making changes in what had become a satisfying idea of what a teacher was and what young children needed. In many ways it was a repudiation of what their highly respected and beloved teachers had reverently taught.[31]

Similar to the circumstances that faced the field's pioneering leaders at the start of the 20th century, new realities at the start of the 21st century create compelling reasons for early care and education leaders to confront the need for adaptive change.

In the decades following the Committee of Nineteen's determinative decisions in 1913, numerous challenges confronted the early care and education field, especially during the 1960s and 1970s with the advent of new research on the impact of early experiences, the onset of early intervention programs, and experimentation with new approaches to early education. In contrast to the challenges presented at the beginning of the 20th century, however, assaults on the field's pedagogy served to coalesce the field, renewing its commitment to, and codification of, developmentally appropriate practice as its pedagogy of choice.[32] Yet the questions posed by Bettye Caldwell during this period regarding the field's own "concept formation" remained largely unanswered.

In the 1990s, in the context of dramatic increases in awareness of and demand for early care and education programs, four adaptive change opportunities emerged. Notably, in 1991, at the onset of this work, Kagan declared, "Never before has the profession had such opportunity, yet been so divided on how to capitalize on the attention and support accorded it."[33]

Each of these efforts generated momentary enthusiasm and focus, and most left a mark on the field. The questions demanding internal resolution remained unanswered, however, and desired transformations failed to materialize. It can be inferred, perhaps, that the field lacked sufficiently compelling reasons to confront and resolve its issues—a dithering that new realities no longer permit.

In 1991, the Carnegie Corporation of New York funded what we consider to be the first of the decade's adaptive change opportunities. It provided funds to NAEYC, the field's largest and most powerful organization, to orchestrate the field's consensus building around the design for a coherent career development framework. Conceptual work initiated by association leaders informed consensus-building efforts focused on crafting a career lattice for early care and education practitioners.[34] At the conclusion of the multiyear funding in 1995, however, limited consensus existed. Although the notion of career lattices has taken hold, a shared career development framework still eludes the field and remains the source of some of our most contentious differences of opinion.

The second effort at adaptive change came in 1996. The Carnegie Corporation of New York, the W. K. Kellogg Foundation, and the Ewing Marion Kauffman Foundation, in conjunction with other foundations, launched the

Quality 2000 Initiative, a 4-year, comprehensive effort to advance new ideas to help define an early care and education system and next-step strategies.[35] Project leaders sought extensive input. Their findings and conclusions significantly inform current conceptualizations of an early care and education system and assisted the field in reaching new levels of sophistication in its thinking. While individual states have used the Quality 2000 and subsequent Policy Matters framework,[36] the hoped-for "domino effect" did not materialize, leaving unresolved many of the field's long-standing differences about its frame of reference.

Also in the mid-1990s, a group composed of national child care advocacy organizations entered into dialogue about what constitutes early care and education—a third effort at adaptive change. It was named the April 19th Group because its first meeting was held on April 19, 1993. The group's goal was the development of a collective advocacy agenda. After issuing a document identifying guiding principles for a child care/early education system, the group dismantled, concluding that it no longer needed to meet. According to Cohen, whether a less competitive relationship among advocacy groups was achieved is unclear. While the work appeared to create a different context for subsequent advocacy efforts, it also left many of the field's leaders disappointed and discouraged about whether the field could move toward a more collaborative and strategic way of doing its work.[37]

Finally, in 1999, the Ewing Marion Kauffman Foundation and Lucile and David Packard Foundation attempted to catalyze the adaptive work needed to create a unified strategy for financing early care and education.[38] Quickly realized, however, was that in the absence of a common definition of what constitutes early care and education, it was impossible to determine what should be financed, much less consider a strategic approach to financing the field's services.

And so, not surprisingly, in 2004, following an assessment of the challenges inherent in the structure of the field's delivery system, Gallagher, Clifford, and Maxwell concluded, "The status quo is not acceptable. . . . if we want true public support for early childhood programs we must mute 'turf protection,' give up the maintenance of autonomy over a select population, and build a coherent system that serves all young children."[39]

FORMING OUR FUTURE

Why, despite its many accomplishments, has the field of early care and education—however one presently defines it—been largely unwilling and/or unable to develop a coherent definition of itself and its work?

Without question, tremendous strides have been made over the past 40 years in reducing the field's fragmentation, elevating the role of advocacy, identifying the essential elements of an early care and education system, and understanding the external forces that impinge upon the ability to effect change on children's behalf. But as understanding of these forces has deepened, we, as a field, have become inclined to rely on this knowledge as an explanation for why we have been unable to effectively advocate for desired changes on behalf of young children and families.

As a field, we also share as organizing principles a belief that children's care and education are inextricably linked and that children's well-being in the present is as important as preparations for their success in the future. A developmental and culturally sensitive approach to early care and education is central to our thinking, as is recognition of the pivotal roles played by families and communities.[40]

These agreed-upon principles can provide a strong basis for our adaptive work. Too often, though, these lofty principles are viewed as sufficient for defining the early care and education field and are used to deflect external attacks and insulate us from making hard choices and engaging in strategic decision making.

We, as authors, recognize that by invoking the need for adaptive leadership work we are entering into uncharted territory. We recognize that by questioning performance, we are challenging the field's current conceptions of its leaders and practitioners. Nonetheless, we believe that significant breakthroughs require the collective and reflective self-examination characteristic of adaptive work. As a field, the time has come to "hold up the mirror" to ourselves.

As strategists Hamel and Prahalad argue, "The future belongs not to those who possess a crystal ball, but to those willing to challenge the biases and prejudices of the establishment."[41] It's time to recognize that "the establishment" can reside within the early care and education field, as well as externally. In the absence of a willingness to name and confront the field's ideologies, cultural norms and practices, and the obstacles they create, we, as authors, predict that opportunities to contribute to restructuring the institutions and programs that serve young children will be limited and that the contributions of the field will be marginalized.

In speaking of the Foundation for Child Development's intent to try to restructure early childhood education in light of its vision for the field, its president Ruby Takanishi noted:

> Message development will entail wading through the swamp of competing and shifting nomenclature for programs serving young children. . . . The confusing and shifting array of names for these programs attests to our

ambivalence and competing ideas about what should be the early education and development experience for children from birth to age eight in the U.S.[42]

Clearly, it is time for those of us who identify with the early care and education field to wade into the swamp, resolve enduring ambivalences about our work, and make decisions about the way forward. We consider the consequences of continued indecision for the field—and most especially for young children—too discouraging to think we would be willing to do otherwise.

CHAPTER 2

New Realities

To state the obvious: The social, economic, and political context for early care and education has changed dramatically over the past 40 years. With the availability of other career options and the field's expansion, well-educated women no longer dominate the field's work force. According to a recent report, the majority of the field's well-educated teachers are approaching the end of their careers, and their less seasoned colleagues have fewer formal qualifications.[1] Thus, the challenge of attracting and holding onto qualified teachers, which has plagued the field for decades, will likely escalate, undermining the field's capacity to elevate and sustain a characteristic level of program quality.

The more dramatic change, though, is the fact that the early care and education field no longer provides its services to children and families in relative obscurity. While still insufficient to the need, early care and education has nonetheless become the recipient of significant public attention and financing. Early care and education has burgeoned into a major industry characterized by a dramatic increase in the quantity of providers and users; expansion of organizations that affiliate themselves with early care and education; allied support from specialized research and advocacy organizations; numerous sector-specific membership organizations; and a growing association with commercial enterprises.

Public acknowledgment of the field's economic impact on communities and its value as an economic investment in future social capital are but two examples of this transformation.[2] The now prevalent presence of mothers in the work force has made the child care sector of interest to prominent investors like Michael Milken and his partners who own Knowledge Learning Corporation, the country's largest for-profit child care company, and to stockholders of Bright Horizons/Family Solutions, an investor-owned company that provides employer-sponsored child care for the country's major corporations. A recent *Child Care Exchange* survey of chief executives of the top 40 for-profit child care providers revealed that most of them reported the highest level of optimism in 5 years.[3] In addition, interest is growing in the idea of prekindergarten providing the official start of children's formal education,[4] and renewed attention is being directed to the importance of kindergarten as a critical transition between early care and education programs and the primary grades.[5]

In 1991, mobilized by a focus on education reform, the nation's governors announced 10 education goals to be achieved by the year 2000, the first of which was "all children will enter school ready to learn."[6] While the other nine goals largely faded from view, the goal of school readiness is widely accepted as a powerful education and school reform strategy.

Sustained interest in children's school readiness can be attributed to several factors. One is public interest kindled by research on early brain development,[7] which has been heightened by well-publicized reports supporting the importance of the first 5 years of children's lives.[8] Carefully disseminated research showing the impact on school achievement of high-quality early childhood education programs for children from low-income families added further visibility, as have reports of reductions in criminal behaviors.[9] More recently, economic cost–benefit studies of high-quality prekindergarten programs have provoked expanded interest by economic, business, and public school leaders in prekindergarten education as a credible way to reduce the achievement gaps between children from low- and middle-income families.[10]

Clearly, early care and education has gained widespread public recognition as a viable solution to the nation's need for a well-prepared work force capable of competing in an increasingly global society. In the process, emphasis is shifting from "early care" to "early education," and from the needs of working families for quality child care to the school-readiness orientation of children.

As repeatedly noted by historians, public interest in early care and education almost always is associated with changing social, political, and economic circumstances and with faith in the capacity of early education to serve as a solution to societal concerns.[11] At the start of the 21st century, this familiar association has reemerged: Policy makers and others again are viewing early care and education as a solution to many of society's pressing economic and social issues.

Unfortunately, history also reveals the frequency with which this relationship concludes without having fundamentally altered the early care and education field's capacity to offer consistently strong programs. Our call for adaptive leadership work is based, in part, on the belief that the current cycle of interest can make an enduring contribution by fostering development of an early care and education system. Seizing this opportunity, however, requires that the field's leadership be able to represent a coherent field of practice—an achievement that requires a field-wide response to the question of what defines and bounds early care and education.

A UNIQUE HISTORICAL MOMENT

The current cycle of interest in early care and education is characterized by a convergence that may be unique in the field's history—a convergence that is simultaneously exciting and worrisome. The qualitative difference from previous cycles of interest comes from the fact that multiple rationales —scientific, social, educational, and economic—have converged to make early care and education of interest to a much broader group of individuals, expanding the range and depth of interest and, potentially, the scope of those who benefit. Unlike earlier cycles of support, current debate includes the extent to which all children, not just children deemed "at risk," should benefit from publicly financed high-quality programs.

This multifaceted public support offers more secure scaffolding than previously has been available to the field—offering a chance to institutionalize a new baseline for early care and education programs. Exciting, therefore, is the possibility of sufficient public interest to make meaningful change in the field's systemic capacity to deliver effective programs and services.

Further evidence of this merger of interests comes from the 40 states that currently invest in prekindergartens, and the level of engagement by business and financial institutions.[12] Across the country, programmatic and policy initiatives abound; these initiatives address diverse facets of early care and education and coexist with state-level work to develop program, content, and early-learning standards.[13]

Acquiescing to the drive for accountability, in large measure because of the connection to financial resources, conversation has shifted from what early care and education programs *do* to the results that they produce, dramatically changing the context for deliberations about the field's purpose, identity, and responsibility. As noted by Richard Clifford:

> Early childhood intervention programs, schools, mental health agencies, and other human service programs are finding themselves under the microscope these days. Lots of different names have been used to justify this scrutiny— accountability, performance-based planning, results orientation, evidence-based practices—but the bottom line is the same. Policy makers are insisting on evidence showing whether public investment in programs for children has achieved its desired results. No longer will it be sufficient to show that programs are meeting established standards for practice or that families are satisfied with services.[14]

Despite many early educators' distaste for the phrase, *school readiness* increasingly defines the "desired result" for early care and education—despite ambiguity regarding the exact meaning of the term. Ironically, the groundswell of support for the contributions of early care and education to children's school readiness represents what potentially is worrisome about current public interest and attention: Worrisome because, as a field, we are unprepared to contribute in an organized and effective way to conversations underway about the results or outcomes for which we should be held accountable and about how they can be achieved. Worrisome because, as a field, we lack the structural, organizational, and management capacity to deliver on the promises being made on our behalf.

FACING NEW REALITIES

Early care and education is being transformed by a changing social and political context, and by public interest in the field. Almost every facet of the field's work is undergoing change: the relationship between "care" and "education"; our independence in deciding what and how we will teach; the rules and regulations that finance and govern our work; and our relationship with the K–12 school system. Appendix A (p. 59) provides a detailed review of early care and education's changing context over the past 25 years.

These changes emerge from driving forces such as the increasing number of women in the labor force, education reform efforts, an ever-expanding global economy, the movement for accountability, and the interests of early care and education's expanded constituency. As noted by one of our interviewees, "The field is changing a lot; the question is: In what direction are we moving?"

Past events have shaped the early care and education field's present realities, and its future will be shaped by present actions. As noted by Peter Drucker in an updated preface to *The New Realities*, key issues of the future are defined by past events. Decision makers "need to factor into their present-day decisions the *future that has already happened*."[15]

Early care and education's "new" realities have been percolating for an extended period of time. By way of example, one can find numerous precursors from the mid-1980s for current debate on public school for 4-year-olds.[16] Some might argue, as did Barbara Biber in 1969, that Head Start deserves credit for what now seems to many to be inevitable: the expansion of K–12 education to pre-K–12.[17]

The link between decisions and choices made in the present to the landscape of the future underscores the importance of collectively doing the adaptive work and futuristic thinking essential to informing the field's prospects. The consequences of choosing to engage or rebuff confrontation with the field's adaptive challenges will influence both the present and future of early care and education. If, as a field, we successfully respond to our adaptive challenges, the decisions and choices we make will be field defining well into the future.

As part of this effort, the broader social, economic, and political context in which early care and education is embedded must be considered. Economic globalization, a new world order, shifting national and state-level politics, changing demographics, an aging population, the rapidity of technological change, rise of the knowledge worker, and concerns related to terrorism come easily to mind as indicators of our present and future. When commenting in 2003 on the next 60 years, Peter Schwartz, a renowned thinker in the area of scenario planning, concluded, "The magnitude of change will be so large and disruptive that, if there should be economic and political stability in the world, it will be a great surprise. The potential for progress is enormous, but the potential for disruption is equally great."[18]

Future prospects for early care and education clearly will be affected by the larger social, economic, and political contexts of which the field is a part. At a minimum, these external contexts have the power to influence the public and private priority given to early care and education and the resources available for its support. External factors can either enhance or restrict the type and range of options that might be considered in planning for the field's future, demanding of us sensitivity to political context as we consider available options. In terms of the field's adaptive work, awareness of this broader context also points to the importance of going beyond what we know—to consider the "art of possibility"[19]—in informing how we approach and ultimately respond to choices embedded in the six field-defining questions.

The field's changing circumstances can largely be explained by five new realities:

1. Early care and education has risen in esteem as a public good.
2. Early care and education has become politicized.
3. Early care and education is expected to produce results.
4. Early care and education must organize itself as an effective delivery system.
5. Early care and education lacks the capacity to meet the public's expectations.

We have been living with the precursors to these new realities for an extended time; discrete events have now gathered sufficient energy and momentum to make them obvious and influential. By naming and making these new realities explicit, we, as authors, hope to increase the field's chances of proactively interacting with them and carefully considering their implications for the decisions and choices needing to be made.

These realities do not replace long-standing facts, such as lack of access by many families, often because of cost, to quality early care and education programs; the need for additional resources to increase and sustain programs of high quality; the absence of career pathways for early educators; and the impact of low compensation on recruiting and retaining competent teaching staff. The field's new realities place these and other long-standing challenges in a different context, however, and alter the way in which their resolution will be debated.

Early Care and Education Has Risen in Esteem as a Public Good

Early care and education has entered the public domain. Engagement by economists and by business, legislative, gubernatorial, and public school leaders makes clear that those of us in the field no longer "own" the issue of early care and education—if ever we did.

This new reality means that we no longer are in dialogue only with ourselves when making decisions about early care and education. It requires us to take others' points of view into account. As expressed by one of our interviewees in speaking to the field's future, "We will not be the people to make these decisions. Early childhood education is a public good. These are public policy decisions. We can inform them, but it's not just about today's young children. It's about the well-being of our country; so the decisions are not ours to make."

Most often, though, consideration of early care and education as a public good is tied to prekindergarten education for 3- to 4-year-olds—which, in turn, is creating tension within the field about programs and services for children from birth to age 3. The amount of publicity accompanying interest in extending the K–12 education system downward to include 4-year-olds, however, masks how much effort is needed even to make consistently high-quality early care and education for 4-year-olds a reality. As reported in the NCEDL Working Paper on the 11-state study of prekindergarten—the most definitive study to date of pre-K education in the United States—most states serve a small percentage of their 4-year-olds and the quality of what is provided is highly variable.[20]

To the extent that most interest in early care and education is directed to public prekindergarten programs for 4-year-olds, and to some 3-year-olds, children from birth to age 3—for whom low-quality early care and education is especially prevalent—are largely absent from the public agenda. Consideration of this age group continues to provoke political fears of encroachment on long-held national values regarding the sanctity of the family and its autonomy in child rearing. As a result, the consensus built during the 1980s regarding the field's unified focus on care *and* education, regardless of program auspice or a child's age, is crumbling, despite policy and community-level efforts to marginalize the fracture. Early care and education is once again being bifurcated, this time on two fronts: the historical fissure between children's "care" and "education" is reemerging, and a dividing line is being drawn between programs for children birth to 3 years and 3- and 4-year-olds.

Additional work obviously is required before it can decisively be said that early care and education has been definitively established as a public good, even for 4-year-olds. Yet public momentum clearly is advancing this new reality and altering the way in which the field considers its work and how others approach us as a field about what we do.

Early Care and Education Has Become Politicized

As a result of its successes, including growing recognition of its public role, early care and education has become a political issue.[21] The issue now engages leaders and decision makers external to early care and education. Governors include prekindergarten education in their campaign platforms[22]; in turn, legislative agendas across the country include early care and education. Prominent civic leaders like *Miami Herald* publisher David Lawrence, Nobel Prize Laureates like James Heckman, and Hollywood actors like Rob Reiner devote time and energies to effecting political change on behalf of young children; and political editorial page columnists, like David Brooks and E. J. Dionne, weigh in on ballot measures on behalf of universal prekindergarten.[23]

This would seem to be a dream come true. Public interest is essential to garnering support for the policies that will be needed to effect systemic change and build support at the community level. Early care and education leaders have wished for the time when sufficient public will would exist to make early care and education a public priority.

Yet with increased public interest and engagement come new leaders, new ideas, new policies, and new pressures. As a result, early care and education increasingly is being defined through often discrete state and local initiatives and often discrete state and federal policies.[24]

Further, early educators are now participants in much larger conversations. Our relative invisibility as decision makers has been altered; our leadership skills are being tested; and our evasiveness regarding what defines and bounds the early care and education field is problematic. While early care and education leaders no longer may need to struggle for visibility and attention, the field's leaders must now learn to manage political conflict,[25] negotiate differing points of view, and compete with other compelling state needs, demanding a much higher level of strategy and skill.

Early Care and Education Is Expected to Produce Results

In return for public and financial support, we are expected to demonstrate, as a field, that our services are effective—that children in early childhood education programs will enter school as effective learners, catalyzing a sequence of positive results that justifies an upfront financial investment in early care and education.

As advocates, we have promised supporters of early care and education clear results: academic success, increased rates of high school graduation, reduced need for special education services, lessened crime, and more productive, tax-paying citizens.[26] The public's expectations for early care and education are fortified further by growing demands for increased performance accountability. Despite attempts to define school readiness as a fusion of ready children, ready families, ready schools, and ready communities,[27] the burden of responsibility has been placed largely on early care and education settings to achieve desired results and often to do so with ill-prepared personnel and limited resources.

This new reality offers the field perhaps the greatest opportunity to inform its future. The means for promoting positive developmental and educational results for children goes to the heart of early care and education's knowledge base. The expectation for results presents an opportunity to use the field's deep knowledge of child development and early childhood education, to protect pedagogical approaches and cultural values that historically have been core to our practice, and to expand our instructional and content expertise.[28]

And the need is great. A January 2005 content analysis of states' early-learning standards revealed the limited extent to which these standards corresponded with the research literature on children's early learning and development.[29] As expressed by an early care and education advocate attacking a newspaper article, "This article does about as good a job as any I have seen to address the unfortunate juxtaposition of the now rapid expansion of preschool and full day kindergarten with the acceleration of expectations and outrageous assessment practices that are accompanying the standards movement. It creates a serious ethical dilemma for us."[30]

Thus, this new reality also brings us face to face with some of the field's most contentious issues. It requires our learning how to defend what we know to be developmentally appropriate, while also confronting our resistance to a changing knowledge base regarding children's capabilities and to escalating expectations for what teachers need to be able to do to promote children's learning and development. It begs the question of whether, as a field, we are willing to hold ourselves responsible for achieving the collective competence required to consistently use our knowledge base.

Early Care and Education Must Organize Itself as an Effective Delivery System

It is well known that the present early care and education delivery system is chaotic, uncoordinated, and of uneven quality. Delivering reliable results —in effect, meeting public expectations for accountability—requires the ability to make high-quality early care and education programs consistently available. It requires putting in place high-quality programs as defined by what research and evaluation have shown are necessary to achieve positive child outcomes.

Achieving consistent program results will necessitate moving beyond a focus on individual programs and individualistic practices to collective adherence to accepted standards,[31] while still encompassing reflective, creative, and culturally sensitive practices. Achieving more even quality across programs will obligate us to design systems that can undergird and promote the consistent provision of early care and education experiences that are associated with children's positive learning outcomes—which we're learning from efforts to take prekindergarten programs to scale is inherently challenging.[32] Governance and accountability structures also will need to be developed.[33]

These demands underscore the inevitability of systems development in early care and education. They also speak to the complexity of system development for a field whose programs are delivered through a mixed market in which a large number of parents are either unable or unwilling to pay for high-quality services.[34] Speaking to the challenges ahead in this regard, one of our interviewees explained, "There will be major losses in status, losses in organizations. To think that we would have a civil conversation is not realistic."

Early Care and Education Lacks the Capacity to Meet the Public's Expectations

The public support being provided to early care and education rests on expectations that it will enable every child to succeed in school and in life. While it is questionable whether this lofty expectation is reasonable in the absence of supportive families, communities, and "ready schools," even partially meeting these expectations requires capacity that the early care and education field currently lacks.

A gap exists between the results attributed to early care and education and our capacity to deliver them. Citing policy makers' reliance on often-quoted longitudinal studies, Morgan and Helburn stated, "It is not generally understood that replicating these positive outcomes will necessitate incorporating the characteristics of the original three studies."[35] This reliance by policy makers is exacerbated by the field's disposition to demand less than what is needed to secure the results evidenced by longitudinal evaluations, in part because of our eagerness to garner political and financial support, and in part because of our hesitation to challenge our colleagues.

This is not the first time that we have experienced a disconnect between what the public thinks it should be receiving and what we as a field are capable of delivering. For example, in the 1960s, the public came to believe that children's brief encounter with a high-quality early care and education program would result in dramatic changes to their developmental trajectory and school readiness, and ultimately would ameliorate poverty. Project Head Start was funded in 1965 based on these expectations and then had to deal with dashed hopes and lessened policy support when evaluation findings concluded that initial gains in cognitive development faded after children's entry into public schools.[36] Even though later research resurrected public support, Head Start's status remains vulnerable, in part because of uneven program results,[37] despite the fact that it can be argued that Head Start is one of the nation's most successful educational programs.

Yet we would contend that a key difference exists between the experience of the late 1960s and the potential in the near future for a divide between public expectations and the field's ability to deliver on them: The stakes are even higher.

In the late 1960s, on the cusp of early care and education's dramatic expansion because of women's entry into the paid labor force, concern revolved around diminished commitment to early intervention and the disappearance of an exciting new program serving a relatively small number of children. Now concerns revolve around the possibility that decades of effort to elevate the importance of early care and education will be dismantled, with consequences for a majority of the nation's children, who now are participants in early care and education programs.

To the extent that as advocates we have extolled the virtues of early care and education and, in order to secure public and financial support, have been less than forthright in articulating what is needed to achieve school readiness—from ourselves as well as from others—we have contributed to creating a field-based performance gap.

CONCERN FOR THE FIELD'S FUTURE

As reviewed above, early care and education has experienced dramatic change during the past 40 years, including the extent to which leaders other than early care and education advocates now tout its contributions. Many, many of the field's leaders deserve accolades for this accomplishment.

The field's successes usually have been achieved against great odds. Many have worked tirelessly, and, according to responses from our interviewees, the field's leaders are tired. Further they are feeling discouraged by the results being achieved with the present approach to change and are worried about the future. (See Appendix B [p. 65] for respondents' comments. Be forewarned: It is not an encouraging or uplifting read. Yet to the extent that acknowledging a problem is a first step toward resolving it, the responses are noteworthy.)

In defining the field's leadership needs, Kagan and Neuman identified the importance of conceptual leadership. Conceptual leadership goes beyond thinking about individual programs to having a sense of the whole. "It is about how we conceptualize our field and how we envision its future and the future of the world today's children will inherit."[38]

The sad truth seems to be that the field is experiencing a dearth of conceptual leadership at a time when it is especially needed. In describing this phenomenon for other fields, Drucker concluded, "Our reality has outgrown our theories."[39] The field's way of being is changing, and we are struggling with how to respond.

No clear vision exists for the future; yet the literature is replete with the importance of having a shared vision in effecting significant change.[40] By arguing for the need to engage in adaptive work, naming the field's adaptive challenges, and offering six field-defining questions, we, as authors, are identifying a way out of this predicament. We are not proposing that adaptive work represents the only response needed to the field's many quandaries. Yet our experiences with significant change efforts, and the responses to our interview and focus group questions, suggest that the early care and education field has yet to fully confront its new realities. The stakes are high for early care and education and for its leaders. Much is expected, and a great deal hinges on how the field chooses to respond.

The field's leadership successes to date have resulted from its unending and unbending efforts to convince others of early care and education's merits. A 2000 Public Agenda report provided an in-depth look at how three groups—parents, employers, and children's advocates—viewed the changing landscape for early care and education. In what they labeled as "the vision that is not there," the report's authors noted that the large majority of experts, advocates, and professionals engaged with early care and education envisioned an approach akin to a European model that offers a universal, national system. The majority of parents, they suggested, did not share this vision.[41] One of us (Stacie) served as one of the two foundation funders for this work. As authors, we both recall the dismissive outrage this report's findings generated from early care and education advocates.

We have concluded that the field's unbending adherence to long-standing positions is no longer productive. We believe that it is time to change and to answer what defines and bounds early care and education as a field—to take a stance on how, as a field, we will effectively deliver on our mission and make a "distinctive impact."[42] We concur with Peter Drucker that "some of the greatest impediments to effectiveness are the slogans, the commitments, the issues of yesterday, which still dominate public discourse, still confine vision."[43]

CHAPTER 3

Necessary Choices

Chapter 1 presented our point of view: We believe the early care and education field is moving toward an uncertain future. In large measure, we think this uncertainty is due to the fact that, as a field, we lack clarity about our purpose, our identity, and our responsibility. The new realities outlined in Chapter 2 make evident that the field is in the midst of disruptive and transforming change. In question is whether the field will play an influential role in shaping the future of its work with children and families.

In order to influence the changes forming the field's future, we argue that the field must enter into adaptive leadership work; it must make decisions and choices that can result in collective answers to the question of its definition and boundaries. These answers are essential to forming a coherent and coordinated system for early care and education. If the field chooses not to engage in this work, we predict that others' answers will be thrust upon it.

Once seemingly the purview of only the early care and education field, the six field-defining questions presented in Chapter 1 have entered into the realm of public debate and policy. In the past, our field made these types of decisions relatively independently of public scrutiny. In line with the field's history, decisions were made by different parts of the field in relative isolation from one another and coexisted in what Clifford has called "parallel play."[1] Now, however, as a result of the field's new realities, decisions and choices that impact the field are being made more often by leaders external to early care and education. Unfortunately, these decisions and choices frequently are made in a way that fails to consider holistically either children or the early care and education field, creating yet another tier of parallel play.

At question is whether, as a field, we can move beyond parallel play. Do we have the courage and tenacity to engage as a collective in the difficult leadership work of adaptive change? Are we willing to make defining decisions and choices to resolve our adaptive challenges, permitting the field to act more effectively on behalf of children's early care and education?

Occupations, like organizations, have distinctive cultures.[2] The early care and education field tends to crave recognition and appreciation for the dedicated service it provides; it also tends to avoid confrontation. As a field, we have a tendency to react defensively to criticism and to feel underappreciated, especially given the fact that the field bears the brunt of the early care and education trilemma (a phrase coined by Gwen Morgan to represent the interrelationship among salaries, affordability, and supply[3]). And rarely does the field initiate the critical self-examination called for by adaptive work. While we, as authors, know that others share our concern, and do not doubt the field's capacity to do this work, we do question whether others share our sense of urgency, without which the field's adaptive work is unlikely to go forward—as was the case with adaptive change opportunities during the 1990s.

Yet *Ready or Not*, early care and education leaders face defining choices. Positioning the field to inform the future of early care and education demands that it engage in a critical appraisal of beliefs, assumptions, past actions, and future possibilities—for the purpose of moving toward a common position on what defines early care and education and the boundaries of the field that delivers its services.

Choices are inevitable. We believe that the status quo is no longer viable and, as a result, acknowledge having preferences regarding the choices to be made. While we have inclinations regarding answers to the six field-defining questions, we do not presume to know what the answers to these questions *should* be. More important—and critical to understand—is that our choices and our decisions are of limited value to the leadership work we are trying to stimulate. Our opinions in this regard merely add two more points of view to the field's literature. Only a field-wide response to the leadership challenge of defining the early care and education field and its boundaries can make the communal difference we are seeking to catalyze.

We wrote this book to provoke forthright, field-wide debate, with the intent of spurring engagement with what we identified in Chapter 1 as the field's two adaptive challenges: a performance gap and a credibility gap. This chapter clarifies these adaptive challenges by providing a beginning exploration of the six field-defining questions.

Making decisions regarding each of the six field-defining questions leads to choices regarding the field's purpose, identity, and willingness to assume responsibility for its work. Ultimately, we believe that these issues confront the field with three choices:

1. *Purpose.* Will the early care and education field have a core focus for its work, *or* will the field's purpose vary based on current societal interests?

2. *Identity*. Will the early care and education field identify and enforce defined criteria to verify the field's collective competence, *or* will the field prioritize open access and inclusion as overarching values?
3. *Responsibility*. Will the early care and education field assume public responsibility for the results of its work, *or* will the field endorse responsibility as the purview of individual programs?

The decision-making options and defining choices are framed as "either–or" because of the field's tendencies to rely on generalities and defer decision making on difficult issues. We know that forced choices do not acknowledge complexities, nuances, or the possibility for "both–and" responses; nor does dichotomous decision making conform to reality. Numerous presentations organized around these field-defining questions, however, have taught us the value of extracting this level of discipline, at least at the front end of the process.

Regardless of the choices ultimately made, trade-offs and consequences—intended and unintended—will be involved. So, to the extent possible, it is important to be conscious of our "choice of errors"[4]—to explicitly recognize what the decisions and choices entail and to be fully aware of the losses they will bring about, as well as of the gains they will produce.

The process of adaptive work will require us to do the hard labor of examining long-standing values and positions, assessing current circumstances, and contemplating possible futures, both the future we wish to create and the future in which the early care and education system may reside. This futuristic aspect of the field's adaptive work is crucial and easily overlooked.

Futurist Peter Schwartz has noted that the future holds many "inevitable surprises"—

> many discontinuities in the economic, political, and social spheres of our world, each one changing the "rules of the game" as it is played today. If anything, there will be more, not fewer surprises in the future, and they will all be interconnected. Together, they will lead us into a world, ten to fifteen years hence, that is fundamentally different from the one we know today. Understanding these inevitable surprises in our future is critical for the decisions we have to make today—whether we are captains of industry, leaders of nations, or simply individuals who care about the future of our families and communities.[5]

Further, it is important that the field sensitize itself to the racial and class differences that, because of its racially tinged history, lie just below the surface of most debate in the field, and can quickly emerge as deeply felt anger and mistrust. Leaders in the field often are unwilling to name the dynamic that is occurring, preferring instead to focus on abstract concepts like "quality for all" and "universal accessibility." Yet as Marilyn Smith noted in her 1987 NAEYC 60th-anniversary address—before concluding with her list of dichotomies that divided early care and education— "For all of the dichotomies I've mentioned, those that undermine and are most destructive to our field and to society are racism and classism."[6]

Predictably, silence about race is not productive and, instead, causes frustrations and communication mishaps. The field's ability to successfully do its adaptive work will require leadership that can acknowledge issues of race and class.

PURPOSE

Three field-defining questions are associated with the issue of purpose:

- What is the early care and education field's defining intent?
- Does the field's intent vary by setting or by auspice (e.g., centers and schools; regulated family child care; license-exempt family, friend, and neighbor care)?
- What chronological span describes the ages of children served (e.g., birth to the start of kindergarten; birth through kindergarten; birth to age 8; prekindergarten through grade 3)?

The overarching choice that confronts the field is whether it wants to be characterized by a primary, core focus *or* whether it prefers that its purpose vary based on current societal interests, thereby possibly gaining the advantages of an opportunistic focus.

The State of "Purpose" in Our Field

Purpose matters. It is the core of mission-driven work. Different purposes define the field's identity in alternative ways; present different demands for the knowledge and skills necessary to perform its work; and generate different expectations for what children should experience. With a defining core, in-depth, shared understanding of purpose can be developed among practitioners, and shifting public and policy priorities are less likely to redirect the field's focus and disrupt or undermine its capacity to do its desired work. On the other hand, the field's ongoing responsiveness to changing societal interests potentially increases its ability to seize new opportunities for marketing its relevance to funders, policy makers, and other decision makers.

Illustrating the intersection of the field's purpose with shifting policy priorities is the Temporary Assistance to Needy Families policy (TANF).[7] The field's flexibility of purpose allowed many early care and education providers to seize the opportunity TANF provided to respond to a policy focus on child care as a facilitator of parental employment. In the process, this policy focus provided a defining purpose for child care and legitimized public-funding parameters that weighted program availability and affordability over program quality, supported minimum public regulation, and minimized the importance of caregiver qualifications.

This policy perspective is driven by the belief that living in economically self-sufficient families is crucial to children's healthy development. Based on this frame of reference, encouraging low-income mothers to transition beyond public support by working in early care and education settings is a smart tactic. So is reliance on the paid service provided by family, friend, and neighbor care, making inconsequential the increasing dominance of the license-exempt child care market.[8]

Yet family, friend, and neighbor care offers considerable variability in quality.[9] Consequently, many of the field's leaders disapprove of the minimal attention this policy framework gives to caregiver qualifications, and the way in which TANF has defined child care's purpose. The presence of a defining core purpose, while reducing the field's responsiveness to new policy incentives, would offer a secure foundation for trying to influence how others define the field's purpose and weight policy parameters.

Currently coexisting with the purpose of early care and education as an enabler of parental employment are political pressures related to school reform that have framed early care and education as preparation for formal schooling, representing yet another example of shifting policy priorities. Many in the field have deep ambivalence about the framework of "school readiness" as a defining purpose. They bemoan the marginalization of developmentally appropriate practice and of babies and toddlers; some question the consequences of failing to attend to the whole child, especially in light of research findings that underscore the importance of social and emotional development to children's learning and school success.[10] Still the field sends a mixed message in this regard because it also welcomes the attention and new resources generated by the school-readiness frame of reference. In the absence of clarity regarding its purpose, the field has lacked the conceptual coherence, as well as the collective strength, to either reject school readiness as the field's primary purpose or to make an expanded definition of school readiness that is inclusive of ready children, ready families, and ready schools and communities more mainstream. Similarly, the field's ambiguity reduces its ability to establish its chronological age boundaries.

As evidenced by these two examples, defining purposes are frequently imposed upon the field by circumstances that, over time, reflect changing societal or political aspirations. In the absence of a defining purpose or a clear strategy for when to harness the potential embedded in shifting priorities, these influences have added to the field's fragmentation, especially when varying purposes have been tied to different program auspices, funding streams, and age groups.

As noted by Morgan and Helburn, "Individual programs, each created to solve a specific problem, include programs for poor children, children of the military, children with special needs, and programs to reform welfare, improve schools, to treat family problems, and to prevent crime and delinquency."[11] As a result of the field's reactive history, programs serving young children have had as their purpose to offer socialization experiences, provide supervised care so parents can work, promote social competence, ameliorate poverty, prevent developmental delays, educate parents, facilitate positive child development, and achieve school readiness. Certainly these purposes can overlap, but they are not equivalent in their rationales, functions, or emphases.

A notable example of how this fluctuation can have disruptive consequences is found in Project Head Start, an initiative that has targeted low-income children since its inception in 1965. Its purpose through these 4 decades of service has varied, emphasizing community empowerment (1960s); social competence (1970s); family support (1980s); family economic self-sufficiency (1980s); and school readiness (1990s). Now, in response to the recent growth in state-funded prekindergarten and the presumption of school readiness as its purpose, Head Start finds itself at the epicenter of current debate about who should be served with public dollars: all children; low-income/special needs children targeted as first in a line that includes all children; or only children identified as having special needs due to their family income or other risk factors. This debate, in turn, raises the question of whether the field's purpose is tied to issues of race and class.

In terms of the field's purpose, at issue is whether the presence of a defining purpose would provide a stabilizing anchor and permit early care and education programs, such as Head Start, to minimize reactivity to fluctuating political interests. Some might argue that shifting political priorities have contributed to the challenge faced by Head Start to develop and evaluate its efficacy. Others might argue that Head Start's flexibility of purpose has contributed to its long-term bipartisan support and survival.

Consequences of Ambiguity About Purpose

Of course, a field's purpose can—and should—shift over time. To act otherwise would indicate stagnation. The issue for early care and education is who makes the choice regarding purpose: Should the choice of purpose be primarily the result of self-determination or the consequence of others' decision making on the field's behalf?

While also recognizing that early care and education programs rarely are limited to singular purposes—and perhaps should be multifaceted—ambiguity about the field's defining purpose confounds our consideration of whether differences among programs in terms of their auspice, setting, ages served, or financing should be associated with different program intentions. Our passion for improving program quality across settings, for example, often leads us to confuse the issue of program quality with program purpose. Similarly aged children are served in different settings: family child care homes, neighbors' and relatives' homes, centers, and schools. Not fully articulated, however, is whether these various settings can or should share the same purpose and whether they are capable of producing similar results.

Too often, our advocacy for the inseparability of care and education blocks our ability to think more analytically about our work and to consider whether the field's defining purpose should, perhaps, be contoured differently depending on the setting and/or sector and/or age of the child. As a result, we deny ourselves the chance to consider whether different settings should have specialized intentions and be associated with different performance expectations.

Ambiguity about purpose also reinforces field-specific sector rivalries. Presently, these rivalries tend to express themselves in terms of "balance of power" among various sectors in the field's mixed delivery system, and anxieties over which sector is "getting the kids" (public schools, family child care, for-profit groups, and so forth). As a result, our energies are directed toward internal battles rather than toward the circumstances that are thwarting the field's ability to deliver competent services. Finally, ambiguity about the field's defining purpose leaves parents and the taxpaying public confused about what they are purchasing. In the absence of a clear purpose statement that is backed by a coherent field of practice, it is legitimate to ask: Who is being served by early care and education? What is the public purchasing when it invests in early care and education?

Defining the Field's Purpose

Should the early care and education field have a core focus for its work or should the field's purpose vary based on timely societal interests? The first choice represents a substantial change from current practice; the second would bring intentionality to the decision to align with shifting priorities.

Making a choice regarding purpose involves decisions about the main rationale for our work and the primary recipient of the benefits reaped from early care and education (see Appendix C, p. 77). In the absence of intentionality, and the continuing presence of ambiguity, our effectiveness as a field, both as practitioners and as strategists, is compromised. If, for example, children were identified as the primary beneficiaries of our work, we would continue our efforts to partner with families, but would not confound partnerships with purpose; whereas if the field's primary service was to families, services to children would be differently positioned and conceptualized.

Leaders external to early care and education understand the importance of clarity regarding mission.[12] If we fail to confront the choices involved in defining purpose and refuse to take a stance, others will make a decision for the field.

IDENTITY

Two field-defining questions are associated with the issue of identity:

- What is the field's distinctive contribution and competence as a collective entity?
- Is early care and education a single/unified field of endeavor or a field comprising subfields (such as health care, for example)?

The overarching choice for the field is whether it wants to identify and enforce defined criteria to verify its collective competence *or* whether it wants to prioritize open access and inclusion as overarching values.

The State of "Identity" in Our Field

Erik Erikson's eight developmental stages revolve around pivotal issues associated with each stage. The pivotal issue for adolescents is labeled Identity vs. Role Confusion. Erikson's description of the issue faced by adolescents is easily transferable to the early care and education field.

> The growing and developing youths, faced with this physiological revolution within them, and with tangible adult tasks ahead of them are now primarily concerned with what they appear to be in the eyes of others as compared to what they feel they are, and with the question of how to connect the roles and skills cultivated earlier with the occupational prototypes of the day.[13]

By substituting "early care and education" for "youths" and deleting "physiological" as a descriptor, we are provided with a depiction of the identity issue facing early care and education in its second century as an organized endeavor. The danger of role confusion and its most prominent manifestation also is applicable: the inability to settle on an occupational identity.[14]

Identity development does not occur in a vacuum; our occupational identity is informed by how our work is viewed by the larger society. The field's fluctuating sense of identity has been defined largely by these influences. In the present, the field's character is being influenced by growing public demand for an effective delivery system, accompanied by increasing public visibility for early care and education.

The NAEYC membership guidelines offer insight into the field's current thinking about affiliation criteria. NAEYC defines itself as the world's largest organization working on behalf of young children and opens its membership to "teachers, administrators, parents, policymakers, and others committed to bringing high-quality early education and care to all young children."[15]

Compare this view with that of the American Nurses Association (ANA), a field similar to early care and education in that nursing has practitioners with varying qualifications. The ANA defines itself as the only full-service professional organization representing the nation's 2.9 million registered nurses. All ANA members must be registered nurses licensed to practice in the United States. In terms of its materials, "ANA recognizes that many students and other individuals who are ineligible to join ANA have an interest in the materials contained within the members' only web site of NursingWorld.org. Individuals may access this site by becoming annual subscribers."[16]

The National Association of Social Workers (NASW) defines itself as the largest membership organization of professional social workers in the world. Its levels of membership include: "regular" members who hold appropriate degrees from recognized social work degree programs and student members. Individuals employed in a social work capacity absent this credential are not eligible for regular membership but may affiliate with the association as associate members.[17]

For multiple reasons, according to Dreeben, a noted sociologist who has extensively studied professionalism and teaching, it is unlikely that any single definition or typology will be found to distinguish professions from nonprofessions. Nonetheless, if one had to choose a single criterion most often associated with a profession, it would be practice based on a learned body of knowledge.[18] It is notable, therefore, that whereas affiliation with ANA and NASW is defined by members' induction into the field via their acquisition of the field's knowledge base and/or license to practice, our field's most prominent membership association defines affiliation by commitment to young children.

In describing NAEYC's organizational framework and leadership on its 75th anniversary, Barbara Bowman noted that NAEYC has established itself as the one organization open to all who take an interest in the field; it has drawn as many individuals and groups as possible under its umbrella.[19] While this approach has reinforced the field's commitment to inclusiveness and the association's role as a consensus builder, it also has permitted the early care and education field to avoid the challenging issue of defining itself and setting its boundaries as an organized field of endeavor.

So perhaps it is not surprising that we found little convergence in the responses during our structured interactions when participants were asked to indicate "who's in and who's out" of the field; to define early care and education as an occupation; to answer what individuals should know and be able to do to claim affiliation with the field; or to identify which settings should be encompassed by the field as an organized entity. The absence of consistent answers to these foundational questions reveals the extent to which the field's occupational identity is characterized by role confusion.

It follows that socialization of individuals who identify with the field is disjointed and uneven. As noted by Bowman, "We have forged little agreement regarding the kind or the amount of training needed by direct service providers, much less by managers, trainers, allied professionals, or supervisors."[20] Given the vagueness regarding how affiliation with the field is demarcated, we lack a formalized process for socializing individuals who self-affiliate with early care and education.

The field's reliance on informal apprenticeship means that individuals generally acquire the field's knowledge, orientation, and values via a process of inference, rather than through an organized program of preparation. As a result, the field's teaching personnel tend to have limited depth of understanding and to lack a coherent conceptual framework to inform their practice with intentionality. Consequently, large numbers of early educators and others who participate in the field tend also to have a fragile loyalty to early care and education, as indicated in part by the field's high turnover rate.[21] Many have limited awareness of the organizational framework that extends beyond the program or age group with which they are associated.

Consequences of Role Confusion

At least three consequences can be attributed to the field's confused identity:

1. *Lack of collective competence.* Inconsistency in individual performance, resulting from unreliable dissemination of the field's knowledge base
2. *A dependability issue.* Uneven quality of early care and education experiences, resulting from a severed connection between the field's knowledge base and its use by practitioners
3. *A fractured field.* Magnification of the field's "parts," which directs attention away from what is shared by the field as a whole

Lack of collective competence. A breach exists between the early care and education field's formal knowledge base and practitioners' familiarity with this knowledge.[22] Dreeben argued that an essential quality of any occupation is its ability to deliver its practice with efficacy. "Indeed, it is difficult to imagine an occupation becoming professionalized without a foundation of efficacious work."[23]

Efficacy, or competence, as defined by Dreeben, refers to the occupation itself, not to individuals. "Competence pertains to a collective entity. What lies behind it are the knowledge and skills available to practitioners, that is the state of the art and its adequacy to meet the demands of the work."[24] While the early care and education field's knowledge base falls short of Dreeben's criteria for occupational competence, the fact that, as a field, we lack a shared expectation for what individuals affiliated with early care and education need to know and be able to do, guarantees that collective competence is beyond our reach—regardless of the sufficiency of our knowledge base and whether the knowledge is acquired prior to or after individuals enter into the field.

Efforts exist to reduce the breach between what is known and what is practiced, and to delineate a common expectation for claiming affiliation with the field. A state-level trend exists toward developing voluntary career lattices for teaching staff and increasing required qualifications for teachers. For example this trend is tied to research on criteria associated with teacher effectiveness,[25] and is augmented by federal[26] mandates and by lawsuits about educational inequity.[27] Significantly, these change efforts are being propelled largely by demands from outside of early care and education. Nonetheless, state child care facility licensing requirements make it possible for virtually anyone to claim affiliation with the early care and education field.

Consequently, upon meeting two early care and education practitioners, little about their job titles or position descriptions would permit assumptions about their educational credentials or skill set. Little has changed since a 1993 national study that depicted the field as a hodgepodge of differing individual licensing standards, training requirements, and training programs.[28] Further, many in the field are comfortable with this status because it marks the field's openness to individuals from diverse backgrounds and experiences.

Our country's changing demographics, and the desire for the field's members to reflect the diversity of the children and families they serve, drive many of us to defend the field's open access as an overriding and defining feature. But we are not on record in this regard, minimizing our ability—if this is our choice—to organize the field based on this as a defining feature.

A dependability issue. Discrepancies in individual performance lead directly to inconsistencies between the field's overall performance and espoused convictions regarding best practice. Pedagogy, in particular the concept of developmentally appropriate practice (DAP), has provided a strong stand-in for the field's occupational identity. Codified in 1986, DAP immediately won field-wide acceptance,[29] an acceptance so pervasive that it has been characterized as "the bible"[30] (though not always expressed as a compliment) and a "virtual litmus test of one's educational philosophy,"[31] even in the face of persistent controversy both within, and external to, the field.[32]

Yet the field's strong identification with developmentally appropriate practice indicates confusion between pedagogy—that is, our preferred teaching methodology—and the defining characteristics that unify us as a field, limiting our openness to other pedagogical practices.

This confusion notwithstanding, the writings of Barbara Biber and others, who during the Progressive Era established the basis for developmentally appropriate practice, make clear that the knowledge and skills required by DAP are extensive.[33] More recently, Barbara Bowman has argued that the study of human development has progressed from a series of beliefs based on observation to a "richly textured knowledge base reflecting research in biology, biochemistry, neurobiology, psychology, linguistics, anthropology, and sociology as well as the pedagogy of teaching academic subjects. To fully understand and translate this complex body of research into practice requires considerable background."[34]

Research affirms the validity of developmentally responsive teaching approaches and their contributions to children's positive development and learning.[35] Yet as a result of the field's uneven socialization practices, practitioners differ widely in their interpretation and application of developmentally appropriate practice, contributing to the uneven program quality available to children and families, and creating a disconnect between what we espouse as a field[36] and what we demonstrate in practice.[37] This disconnect is one of the factors that places the field's integrity at risk, especially at a time when accountability for public investments is increasingly the norm.

The development and implementation of standards of all kinds is considered a primary lever for altering this state of affairs. In response, Margie Carter has passionately questioned, "Standards or standardization: Where are we going? . . . Whose interests are being served?"[38] While, as authors, we contend that the early care and education field must confront a choice regarding its public responsibility—and a decision regarding the use of standards is inevitably a part of this choice—Carter's plea underscores the urgency of responding to the field's adaptive challenges so we can become more effective leaders who can influence the function and potential of the standards movement and other external influences on our work.

A fractured field. Age of the child, program sector, and auspice—not the field as a whole—tend to frame individuals' occupational identity and allegiances. An individual working in early care and education is more likely to say, "I work in Head Start," or to mention one of the field's sectors, than to say, "I work in the field of early care and education." Identity with an individual component of the field, rather than with the field as a whole, has spawned rivalries and differences in employment and career trajectories. The result has been creation of an implicit hierarchical pecking order that differently values service by age groups (e.g., infants vs. kindergarteners), by settings (e.g., family child care vs. schools), and by auspice (e.g., for profit vs. not-for-profit). The field's work has been compartmentalized, and competition among the field's "parts" undermines creation of a shared frame of reference, creating barriers to comprehensive planning efforts[39]—and to a coherent identity as a field of endeavor.

Determining Our Occupational Identity

As a field, will we identify and enforce defined criteria to verify our collective competence, *or* will we prioritize open access and inclusion as overarching values?

Any serious engagement with this choice will necessitate making difficult decisions regarding what defines our collective identity as a specialized endeavor and what it is about our work that brings distinctive value to children, families, and society overall (see Appendix C, p. 78). Verifying our distinctive contribution is essential to securing recognition as a public good. Confronting the issue of the field's identity will require decisions about how we will characterize our identity, the core knowledge and skills needed by practitioners for collective competence, and the program parameters and structure that bound the field so form can follow function.

RESPONSIBILITY

A single field-defining question is associated with the issue of responsibility:

- To what extent are we, as a field, willing to hold ourselves accountable to one another and to be held publicly accountable for results
  in return for the autonomy to deliver programming based on the
  field's knowledge base?

The overarching choice is whether, as a field, we will choose to assume
public responsibility for the results of our work *or* whether we will endorse
responsibility as the purview of individual programs.

The State of "Responsibility" in Our Field

The five new realities outlined in Chapter 2 make the issue of responsibility especially high stakes. In return for public and financial support, the
early care and education field is expected to demonstrate collective competence—to give evidence of its ability to deliver reliable services of high
quality that consistently produce positive results, assuring the public that
its investments in early care and education are worthwhile.

    As early care and education advocates, we have promised supporters
of early care and education clear results: academic success, increased rates
of high school graduation, reduced need for special education services,
lessened crime, and more productive, tax-paying citizens.[40] As service
providers, we have been less forthcoming.

    The issue of responsibility is so tantamount because, as a field, we lack
an organizing framework for responding to questions about our collective
responsibility to society, to families, and to children, or even to one another
as members of an organized occupation. Instead, we have relied on landmark studies demonstrating the effectiveness of high-quality early care and
education settings as a proxy. But states too rarely include the program
elements that landmark studies used to achieve their impressive results
(e.g., parent involvement, home visits, highly credentialed staff, and low
ratios).[41] Further, when advocating, the field too often prioritizes the availability of new funding and expanded programming over policy grounded
in research. It tends to distance itself from the performance risks associated with aligning what is known about effective programs with policies
designed to achieve their results.

    Yet the field is increasingly the recipient of new policy demands for
increased accountability. For example, the Head Start Child Outcomes
Framework includes 13 mandated learning indicators, such as the quan-

tity of numbers and letters that Head Start graduates should know. Additionally, in April 2002, the Bush Administration launched a National Reporting System assessment tool—a tool that many in the field believe lacks credibility because it is not coupled with children's meaningful activities.[42] Many states have instituted content standards that document what children should be learning, as well as early-learning standards that express what children are expected to know and be able to do.[43]

This new reality brings us face to face with long-standing conflicts. It requires us to confront our resistance to a changing knowledge base regarding what children are capable of knowing and our discomfort with escalating expectations for what teachers need to know and be able to do to support children's learning and development. It requires us to examine the discrepancy between our rhetoric on diversity as an asset and the coexisting attitude that the field's diversity is a hindrance to having higher expectations for personnel. Accountability issues beg the question of whether we are willing to hold ourselves responsible for achieving the collective competence required to consistently apply our knowledge base.

Beyond state facility licensing requirements, we are accustomed as a field to determining our level of responsibility. While the impact of Head Start programs continues to be debated, their mandatory, standardized, public definition of program quality is an exception within the field. (Federally legislated Program Performance Standards for Head Start have been in place since 1970.[44]) To the extent that NAEYC's Code of Ethical Conduct and Statement of Commitment[45] represents a position on ethical behavior, the field is open to accusations of malpractice. While an incredibly strong and harsh assertion, evoking the possibility of "malpractice" names the stakes associated with this issue.

Increasingly, programs may choose to adhere to the many voluntary systems of accountability, such as states' quality-rating systems and national associations' program accreditation systems. Yet even when accountability is voluntary, the field often hesitates to assume responsibility for its actions and performance—to put in place high-quality programs as defined by what research and evaluation have shown are necessary for achieving positive learning and developmental outcomes for children.

The field's hesitancy to hold itself accountable to a level of quality that increases the chances programs will deliver results consistent with landmark studies was evident during NAEYC's reinvention from 2000 to 2005 of its early childhood program accreditation system. As participants in this process, we experienced the field's contradictory responses: acknowledgment of the validity of proposed accreditation criteria on the one hand and resistance to performing at a level reflective of them on the other. Rather than directing attention to what was needed so programs could meet these performance expectations, energies were directed mostly to diluting the criteria. While acknowledging the legitimacy of expressed concerns, we also recognize the contradiction inherent in deferring program accountability for performing at a level aligned with the field's knowledge base, while simultaneously advocating for public support on the strength of that same knowledge base.

Given this state of affairs, it is to be expected that evaluation studies repeatedly document the uneven quality of early care and education programs.[46] Further, as documented by Herzenberg, Price, and Bradley, younger teachers, especially those working in community-based settings, are less likely than their older counterparts to be college educated—in marked contrast to the nation's work force as a whole.[47] This finding implies that the field's intellectual range may be declining and raises additional concerns regarding the field's ability to deliver a quality of services aligned with public expectations.

Consequences of Avoiding Responsibility

At least two consequences result from avoiding responsibility: missed opportunities for children and postponed responsibility.

Missed opportunities for children. If the field is to achieve consistent and high-level program results, it will be necessary to move beyond a focus on individual programs, artistic practitioners, and idiosyncratic practices, and toward collective adherence to accepted standards. Achieving more constant quality across programs will obligate us to design an early care and education system that can undergird and promote consistent provision of early-learning experiences that are associated with children's positive learning and development.

Yet, the most typical field-wide response to overall low performance is advocacy for greater public investment. While funding is unquestionably necessary, relating poor performance entirely to such external factors tends to shift responsibility outside of the field. Numerous social and economic conditions, such as inadequate compensation, a highly competitive marketplace, and high staff turnover rates, provide both rationale and justification for the field's reluctance to assume more public responsibility. Even though the field clearly is underresourced, as authors, we question whether additional resources, in the absence of decisions regarding the field's collective responsibility, can dramatically change results. Further, in the face of new realities, the field increasingly is at risk of being the recipient of the public's externally imposed expectations.

Ultimately, though, bypassing a choice of collective responsibility for our work means we will miss, as a field, the opportunity to more widely and effectively interrupt the trajectories of differential outcomes for children. The benefits of high-quality early care and education are well established, especially for low-income children and children of color. Well before kindergarten, sizeable developmental gaps exist among children, often because of issues tied to race, class, and ethnicity.[48] This circumstance offers the early care and education field an unmistakable opportunity to influence children's lives. To the extent that poor children and children of color are served by a field that avoids collective responsibility and fears performance accountability, we squander the privilege to be agents on behalf of equity and social justice.

Postponed accountability. The field has effectively cited the results from landmark studies as evidence of its efficacy; legislators and business leaders now quote these studies as a basis for their support. Children typically are not enrolled in these types of programs, however, and the difference in this regard is seldom clarified or understood. We have, in essence, severed connections between what our work is capable of producing when certain conditions are in place and what we are willing to hold ourselves accountable for doing. The field has implied that it can and will deliver outcomes similar to those in the landmark studies that are cited so frequently. By not being more forthright about what the majority of our programs can be expected to deliver in terms of results, we have garnered public and legislative support. The field must now understand that it has postponed to an unspecified future date—but not eliminated—questions of accountability. The federal imposition of mandates regarding the numbers and letters children in Head Start must learn might be considered an isolated event resulting from unique circumstances or as an omen for the future. As authors, we think it wise to regard creation of this policy as a cautionary tale.

Determining Our Responsibilities

The choice of whether to assume collective and public responsibility for the field's performance will be intertwined with the choices and decisions the field makes regarding its purpose and identity. Unlike times in the past, however, when intense public interest in the field's work dissipated over time, the field's new realities suggest deeper "investor" commitment to early care and education. It is our sense as authors that these investors, unlike in times past, are more likely to stay with the issue and move forward with an agenda without us. When ascertaining decision elements related to the assumption of collective responsibility, careful consideration needs to be given to what is at stake (see Appendix C, p. 79).

CALLING THE QUESTION

We have characterized the early care and education field as having an ambiguous purpose, as suffering from role confusion, and as reluctant to assume collective responsibility for its work. In the absence of engaging in field-wide adaptive work and confronting the decisions and choices associated with the issues of purpose, identity, and responsibility, we fear that the field will limit its opportunities to influence the future for children and early care and education.

We challenge the field to enter into adaptive leadership work, to generate field-wide debate and consensus building, and to be courageous. We call the question: What defines and bounds early care and education as a field?

CHAPTER 4

Leading by Changing

A prominent strategic thinker in our field surprised herself when she responded to one of our interview questions by saying, "I have no idea what we should do next."

We do. We think the early care and education field should engage in leadership work to answer the central question: "What defines and bounds early care and education as a field?" In the absence of a coherent and field-wide answer to this defining question, we believe the field's ability to serve children well, and to advocate effectively on behalf of early care and education, is severely compromised.

We have argued that adaptive leadership work, as defined by Ron Heifetz and his colleagues,[1] offers a conceptual framework for understanding the field's challenges and for the necessity of field-wide engagement to resolve them. Adaptive work describes a particular "species" of leadership. If pursued, the field will need to make fundamental choices about its work in order to reach a shared point of view regarding the three paramount issues of purpose, identity, and responsibility, plus how to move forward with the decisions and choices that have been made. Importantly, this work also "must track the contours of reality; it has to have accuracy, and not simply imagination and appeal."[2]

Adaptive work is about change—about changing how we approach our work, our relationship with one another, and our relationship with policy makers and other decision makers. It is a form of leadership that demands learning "to address the conflicts in the values people hold, or to diminish the gap between the values people stand for and the reality they face."[3] Adaptive leadership work strives to close the distance between people's espoused values and their actual behaviors, work that by definition often calls for painful trade-offs.[4]

We have argued that the early care and education field faces two adaptive challenges: a performance gap, between articulation of high standards and uneven quality in practice, and a credibility gap, created by our reluctance to confront the field's self-protective conduct as it relates to our collective competence.

We have built the case for these gaps as adaptive leadership challenges by relying on the distinction between technical problems and adaptive challenges—between problems with preexisting solutions, regardless of the level of implementation difficulty, and challenges that lack known answers. In the absence of known answers, those who have a stake in the issue have to confront conflicting values and work through differences to create solutions that "are better adapted to the politics, culture, and history of their situation."[5]

Technical answers do not exist for the two adaptive challenges that we have identified the field as having. In fact, the answers are unknown. Will we, as a field, step forward to answer them? If we wish to be the ones to answer the central question of what defines and bounds early care and education as a field, we must tackle these challenges.

ADAPTIVE WORK

Given its distinctive character, adaptive leadership does not direct individuals to respond in specified ways. Consistent with dynamic views on leadership, its focus is less on leadership characteristics and on leadership conferred by a person's position, and more on leadership as an activity, on mobilizing people to tackle difficult problems, and on creating the conditions for doing the adaptive work necessary to achieve progress.[6] Adaptive work, therefore, has two components

1. The learning required by those of us who must come together to resolve internal contradictions that are creating discrepancies between the field's espoused values and its actual behaviors
2. Using knowledge about adaptive pressures and dynamics so we can confront necessary trade-offs and learn to behave differently[7]

As a result, the leadership work we are trying to catalyze is a collective activity that needs to engage a wide range of people who are in varied positions and who have diverse points of contact with the field's adaptive challenges—rather than the conveyance of solutions from anointed leaders or leaders in positions of authority.

By choosing to engage in adaptive work, the early care and education leadership will be choosing to lead on behalf of the field and its constituencies in a new way. Senge defines this kind of leadership as the "capacity of a human community to shape its future, to sustain significant change."[8]

If done well, the field's approach to its adaptive work can respond not only to its adaptive challenges but also to building new leadership capacity and increased leadership effectiveness.

PREPARING FOR ADAPTIVE WORK

Adaptive leadership work starts with focusing attention—with getting people to pay attention to the issue. By each of us initiating discussions and debates in towns and cities across the United States, we can begin the change process. The framing question, "What defines and bounds early care and education as a field?" and the six field-defining questions with their decision elements can be used to focus participants' attention on the field's issues.

Building Awareness of the Issues

Laying the groundwork for adaptive work begins with building awareness. This process can begin by organizing small groups of people and asking them to think about the field's new realities and their implications, distinguishing between technical problems and adaptive challenges, and moving toward acknowledgment of the field's two adaptive challenges. It will be important to keep the intent of these informal discussions in the forefront: to focus attention and to begin self-organizing for adaptive work.

In the process, new insights about the field's adaptive challenges likely will emerge, and new ways of thinking about the field's choices may become evident. Participants may even reformulate the choices, rework the field-defining questions, and add to and subtract from the decision elements.

To be productive, these conversations should include divergent perspectives, as well as individuals who are willing to bring these differences out into the open. Conflict is important in adaptive work; it helps make contradictory values evident and available for the work at hand. Eliciting conflicting points of view in a way that promotes shared learning can be difficult for any field, but especially for ours. The field tends to avoid conflict and often does so by relying on undefined terms, such as *high quality* and *universal*, or on abstract agreements about our shared work, such as "We all want to do what is best for children," or "We care about the whole child." The field has been behaving in this way for so long, it may not even be aware of the avoidance function that this habit performs. While useful for masking our fractures and maintaining a sense of harmony, these generalizations can undermine adaptive work by permitting the field to avoid the hard task of identifying and understanding its differences.

Those who facilitate these conversations (and there may even be value in using the services of a professional facilitator) need to be familiar with group dynamics and the unique qualities of adaptive work. Insecurities and accompanying anxieties may become high once colleagues engage with these issues. Further, where these conversations will lead is an unknown, and closure may not be available by a meeting's end, adding to the possible sense of discomfort.

Facilitating adaptive work involves helping participants "hold" the range of feelings that will surface, mediating conflict among stakeholders, and generating and maintaining what Heifetz calls productive distress. The leadership work involves surfacing conflicts and then making sure that they don't spin out of control. It requires skillfully using tensions to mobilize adaptive work, while also ensuring that tension levels do not become overwhelming. Adaptive leadership work uses all of these situations to promote new learning and to facilitate progress toward resolving an adaptive challenge.[9]

Recognizing Adaptive Work as Field-Wide Work

Indicative of the field's once small size, as well as a dearth of institutional leadership, early care and education leaders emerged for the most part on the merits of their personal capabilities. Despite dramatic changes in the field, its leadership has remained relatively insular and static. Now increasingly evident is the way in which this leadership pattern is creating barriers to developing the community of leaders our future requires. As expressed by one of our interviewees: "I see older leaders anxious not to lose their power to younger leaders. Those 'behind us' are less prepared, and less prepared to lead. There are no second lieutenants."

Yet field-wide leadership will be essential if the field is to fully understand and respond to its two adaptive challenges. In the absence of field-wide leadership representing a wide range of voices, the field will truncate its learning process and undermine its chances of cultivating a collective and authentic multicultural voice.

Adaptive change results in new values and behaviors that can provide a basis for shaping a different future. These changes originate from each of us—individually and collectively. This is why responding to the field's adaptive challenges should be our work and why, in order to result in "profound change,"[10] an inclusive process must be used.

Our field includes individuals with a wide range of ethnic, racial, and linguistic backgrounds.[11] Most recently, as a result of expansion of the Temporary Assistance to Needy Families policy, license-exempt child care, in particular, has become dramatically more diverse in terms of language, race, ethnicity, formal education, and occupational identity.[12] The full range of these voices must be included in our adaptive work. We also should be sensitive to the fact that accomplished Asian, Black, and Latino professionals repeatedly express a sense of professional isolation and marginalization.[13]

At the same time, the field needs to prepare itself to confront the discord its diverse composition can provoke. Presently, the field's diversity is framed as both an asset *and* a hindrance to advancement. Our country's changing demographics, and our desire for the field's members to reflect the diversity of the children and families being served, drive many to defend the field's open access as an overriding and defining feature. It is not uncommon, therefore, to hear as a point of view that a commitment to workforce diversity is incompatible with instituting higher entry standards. Sometimes the reply will be, "Whose children, then, will be denied access to qualified teachers?" or "Are you suggesting that teachers of color are not capable of achieving higher qualifications?" More often, these responses remain unexpressed, and participants experience the sense of being silenced. Silence about race and class, however, inevitably will impede adaptive change.

Anticipating the racial and class overtones of the field's adaptive work, it is worth noting that, from our experiences, the leadership that advocates for "all children" being served is predominately White and middle class. This feature stands in marked contrast with the more racially, linguistically, and economically diverse population served by targeted programs such as Head Start.[14]

Fortunately, the early care and education field can turn to existing work to assist it with addressing issues of race and class in the context of its adaptive work. The "Children of 2010" project, for example, facilitated difficult conversations by framing issues of diversity in the context of democratic principles and stewardship of our common, national future, contending that our 21st-century democracy will require an unprecedented level of cooperation, communication, and teamwork among people who are different. Relying on fact finding, disclosing hidden assumptions, and seeking additional points of view further minimized the risks of engaging with sensitive issues.[15]

Identifying Decision-Making Archetypes

In Chapter 3, we presented the significant choices and decisions that the field's adaptive work will entail. Based on our analysis of the field's decision making, we predict that it will rely on four approaches if it undertakes adaptive work:

1. Protecting historically valued positions
2. Working to maintain equilibrium
3. Pursuing the field's new realities as strategic opportunities to secure improvements
4. Focusing on conditions that can promote sustainable results

We have conceived of these four approaches to decision making as archetypes and have labeled them guardians, accommodators, entrepreneurs, and architects (see Table 4.1). As approaches to decision making, these archetypes are generalities. No one approach, by itself, fully responds to the range and complexity of issues that are part of the field's adaptive work.

Our characterizations are intentionally stark to distinguish among them. Each individual also may use more than one decision-making approach, depending on the issues involved. As described by Mayo and Nohria, context is critical to understanding the leadership styles used by different leadership types.[16] Leaders with dissimilar styles differently recognize contextual opportunities and also differently influence their context.

No one of our suggested approaches to decision making is necessarily better than another. It is failing to take context into consideration, or as a field relying solely on one approach to decision making, that is limiting. Consequently, all four of these decision-making archetypes are needed for the adaptive work ahead. Each approach has the potential for positive and negative possibilities, depending on the specifics that define the issue at hand. Our intent in identifying these four archetypes is to illuminate how we might engage with the choices and decisions ahead—assuming that as a field we choose to enter into adaptive leadership work.

MOBILIZING THE EARLY CARE AND EDUCATION FIELD FOR ADAPTIVE CHANGE

As already noted, a central characteristic of adaptive work is clearly recognizing and acting on the fact that those who have possession of the adaptive challenge should be the ones to do the adaptive work. The early care and education field should create and implement the solutions because the roots of the problems are found in our attitudes and behaviors. If we as a field want to take the lead in answering the question of what defines and bounds early care and education, we must take responsibility for resolving our adaptive challenges.

Doing this adaptive work will require the field to develop the capacity to identify what is valuable; reflect on the costs and consequences asso-

Table 4.1. Archetypes for decision making in early care and education: Coexisting approaches.

	Guardians	Accommodators	Entrepreneurs	Architects
Worldview	Protective	Realistic	Opportunistic	Holistic
Motivating factor	Consistency; programmatic stability	Maintaining equilibrium; realism	Strategic improvements; competitive advantage	Catalyzing change through effective policy
Approach to change	Wary; grounded in field's history	Pragmatic; consensus building	Welcoming and anticipatory	Long-term view; focused on creating conditions for sustainable results
Action orientation	Cautious; interested in sustaining historical values	Incremental; moves to the "middle" to create a new mainstream	Results-oriented	Future-oriented; proactive
Primary slant for thinking about purpose	Protects traditional views of children and their growth	Sensitive to ideas at the center of traditional and emerging viewpoints	Pursues new frames of reference that will promote innovative opportunities	Seeks hidden potential that can promote new commitments to children
Primary slant for thinking about the field's identity	Protects the field's traditional, charitable mission to support children and families	Sensitive to field's traditional, charitable mission to support children and families when adjusting to the contemporary context	Pursues new thinking in order to expand horizons and future possibilities	Seeks essential/core elements that promote resilience in changing circumstances
Primary slant for thinking about the field's responsibility	Protects the child and her development	Sensitive to the interface between child's development and public expectations	Responds to public opinion	Seeks alignment between intentions and results

ciated with various options; and work through conflicts that will need to be addressed if we are to find collective answers to the field's adaptive challenges.[17] Critically, it requires:

- Learning to be attentive and responsive so the conditions necessary for change can be fostered
- Learning to build consensus around possible answers
- Learning what will be needed to carry the results forward[18]

A brief history of previous attempts by the field to engage in adaptive work was offered in Chapter 1. All of these attempts added to the field's self-knowledge, but with the exception of the work of the Committee of Nineteen, none of them gathered sufficient momentum to affect transformative change within the field.

A sense of urgency is necessary for mobilizing change.[19] The field's five new realities, outlined in Chapter 2, explain why it no longer can afford to delay engaging with the task of coalescing around a common set of definitions and boundaries for its collective work as a field—especially if we wish to serve children well and perform effectively as early care and education advocates.

Heifetz and others speak to the importance, once the need for adaptive work has been identified, of systematically ripening an issue: of focusing attention, building capacity to do the work, managing the tensions that naturally emerge from engaging with difficult choices, and confronting the losses that these choices entail.[20] Toward this end, we have identified for the field its two adaptive challenges and forecast the consequences that will result if, as a field, we choose to bypass the adaptive changes they necessitate. We also have framed the field's challenges in terms of the opportunities they present, as well as their difficulties.

Before arriving at the point of doing adaptive leadership work, the field first must acknowledge its adaptive challenges and recognize its tendency to treat them as if they were technical problems with routine solutions, such as increased funding, improved messaging, and/or new demonstration projects. It must engage in the very hard work of confronting the gaps between espoused values and actual behaviors. Reaching this milestone will require that many others in the field join with us, as authors, in calling the question: What defines and bounds early care and education as a field? (See Figure 4.1.)

Much is at stake for the early care and education field:

- Its ability to state clearly who we are and what we do
- Cohesion as a field

Figure 4.1. Adaptive challenges of the early care and education field.

THE FIELD'S TWO ADAPTIVE CHALLENGES: GAPS BETWEEN ESPOUSED VALUES AND BEHAVIORS

THE PERFORMANCE GAP: The gap between the field's expressed commitment to children's high-quality early care and education and its uneven collective competence

THE CREDIBILITY GAP: The gap between the desire to be recognized as leaders on behalf of early care and education and the field's self-protective behaviors

THE CENTRAL QUESTION

What defines and bounds early care and education as a field?

THE FIELD'S DEFINING ISSUES, QUESTIONS, AND CHOICES

PURPOSE

1. What is the early care and education field's defining intent?
2. Does the field's intent vary by setting or by auspice (e.g., centers and schools; regulated family child care; license-exempt family, friend, and neighbor care)?
3. What chronological span describes the ages of children served (e.g., birth to the start of kindergarten; birth through kindergarten; birth to age 8; prekindergarten through grade 3)?

CHOICE: Will the early care and education field have a core focus for its work, *or* will the field's purpose vary based on current societal interests?

IDENTITY

4. What is the field's distinctive contribution and competence as a collective entity?
5. Is early care and education a single/unified field of endeavor or a field comprising organized subfields (such as health care, for example)?

CHOICE: Will the early care and education field identify and enforce defined criteria to verify its collective competence, *or* will the field prioritize open access and inclusion as overarching values?

RESPONSIBILITY

6. To what extent are we, as a field, willing to hold ourselves accountable to one another and to be held publicly accountable for results in return for the autonomy to deliver programming based on the field's knowledge base?

CHOICE: Will the early care and education field assume public responsibility for the results of its work, *or* will the field endorse responsibility as the purview of individual programs?

- The capacity to fulfill the purpose(s) we articulate
- Collective competence capable of providing a dependable level of program quality
- The public respect that comes from a mutually agreed-upon "contractual" relationship that is contingent on the field's accepting responsibility for the results of its work

If taken to heart, the questions we are posing, and the field-wide work we are proposing, can revolutionize the early care and education field, not unlike the results of the adaptive leadership work undertaken by the Committee of Nineteen that transformed the field's approach to its practice at the beginning of the 20th century.

For this potential to be realized, an explicit, nationwide process eventually will be needed for orchestrating and coordinating the work and for acting on the choices the field makes. We are optimistic that organizational leadership will emerge once the field's adaptive challenges are widely acknowledged and a groundswell of support exists for engaging in the necessary adaptive work.

The early care and education field cannot be protected from change. The primary purpose of this book has been to identify and focus the field's attention on its adaptive challenges, to make the field aware of the leadership that is needed, and to invite others to join with us in "calling the question." Responding to this call requires the conviction that new thinking and behavior will allow the field to form its future in exciting ways—and, importantly, in ways that make a difference for the well-being of children and for early care and education.

Ready or Not, the field of early care and education faces new realities. The field's leadership work begins with our collective involvement and commitment to change. As authors, we are energized by the work and potential that lie ahead.

APPENDIX A

Early Care
and Education's
Changing Landscape

The context for early care and education is changing. This changing context is being driven by external factors, including the five new realities presented in Chapter 2. In Table A.1, we provide concrete evidence of the changing landscape by presenting the dominant context for early care and education between 1980 and 1999 and juxtaposing it with the field's emerging context as of 2000. We do not presume to have identified all of the changes that have taken place since the start of the 1980s, the year we selected as the baseline for our comparison nor are we suggesting that the changes between these time periods are absolute.

The examples identified were selected because (1) they portray a snapshot of early care and education at two different points in time and (2) they illuminate issues that need to be considered in responding to the six field-defining questions (see Chapter 1). We recognize that sometimes it is only the conversation that has changed, not the reality of children's daily experiences. Nonetheless, the shift in rhetoric creates a new frame for the field's decision making during this time of system building.

Our examples are organized by five categories:

- Views on children and their early learning
- External interest in early care and education
- Characteristics of early care and education programs and services
- Descriptors of the early care and education field
- Leadership dimensions

Table A.1. The context for early care and education.

	Prior Context (1980s and Forward)	Emerging Context (2000 and Forward)
VIEWS ON CHILDREN AND THEIR EARLY LEARNING		
View of children	Children follow a "natural" developmental trajectory that is enhanced by a nurturing and supportive learning environment.	Young children are voracious learners capable of learning much more than previously thought. Renewed focus on early experiences as predictive of future success. Access to new technology is changing children's daily experiences and interests.
Purpose of early care and education	Developing the "whole child" for some children; supporting parental employment for others. Alleviating poverty.	School readiness. Preparation for success in a global economy. Alleviating achievement gaps.
EXTERNAL INTEREST IN EARLY CARE AND EDUCATION		
Public interest	Public interest in early care and education dominated by race and class issues. Early care and education viewed as the private responsibility of families.	High interest in prekindergarten for 4-year-olds, especially for children believed at risk for school failure. Recognition of early care and education as means for reducing the achievement gap between low- and high-performing students. Continuing resistance to publicly supported programs for children birth to age 3.
Financing	Child care costs determined primarily by families' ability to pay. Public subsidies available for low-income families that meet financial thresholds established by individual states.	Diversified categorical public funding tied to program type. Extent of federal and state investment has escalated since 1990; the availability of private support is limited.
Government support	Government engagement is primarily at the federal level and tied to categorical policy interests.	Increasing state-level funding support for prekindergarten and quality-improvement efforts through standard setting and quality-rating systems.
Business as child care provider	Growing number of businesses willing to serve as primary provider of services in order to recruit and retain a strong work force.	Decrease in interest by businesses in serving as a primary provider of services because new options are available for supporting employee needs through subcontracts and Employer Assistance Programs.
Investor interest	Marginal interest by investors because profit margin considered too narrow.	Target of corporate traders, and of publishers and toy companies. Owners of early care and education services and products traded on New York Stock Exchange. Emergent consolidation of small franchises.

Philanthropic interest	Strong interest from a core group of national foundations with increasing involvement from regional foundations; Early Childhood Funders Collaborative, a group of national and regional philanthropists with strategic interests in early care and education, launched in 1995.	Investments come from a select group of national foundations with highly targeted interests and from regional and local foundations interested in supporting direct services and/or change efforts in their home communities.

CHARACTERISTICS OF EARLY CARE AND EDUCATION PROGRAMS AND SERVICES

Sponsorship	Wide array of sponsorship: public and private; faith-based; not-for-profit and for-profit. Program identity tied to sponsorship. Available programs primarily child care, Head Start, and preschool. Numerous auxiliary services emerge to provide program support services.	Program auspices increasingly less relevant as programs and services become more diversified, and level of service becomes more significant than auspice. Serving the "whole child" through linkages with related services, such as physical and mental health, becomes more prominent issue.
Delivery system	Decentralized and fragmented. Programs individually owned and managed.	Center-based programs increasingly centralized: managed by school districts, multipurpose nonprofit agencies, the military, and corporate structures such as Bright Horizons Family Solutions and Knowledge Learning Corporation. Expanded interest in family, friend, and neighbor care, accompanied by uncertainty regarding its appropriate relationship to regulated settings. Increasing participation by charter schools. Growing responsiveness to market system.
Consumer/ purchaser demand for program quality	Half-day enriching preschool experience of interest to middle-class families for purposes of socialization. Child care a necessity for mothers employed outside of the home, and pragmatic needs (e.g., cost and availability) drive parental choice. Onset of efforts to provide information to families on program quality; efforts to provide information hampered by fear of discrediting programs and promoting parental anxiety.	Increasing demand for school-readiness orientation from employers, policy makers, and educational and business leaders who view early care and education as solution to achievement gap and development of human capital. Emergence of quality-rating systems by states to market higher quality child care programs to parents and other purchasers.

(continued)

Table A.1. *(continued)*

	Prior Context *(1980s and Forward)*	*Emerging Context* *(2000 and Forward)*
Sector cohesion	Programmatic and funding fragmentation linked to program identity and categorical funding. Efforts to transcend split between "care" and "education" sectors begin to take hold.	Reemergence, educationally and programmatically, of distinctive—versus complementary—functions of child care and early education. Sectors increasingly competitive in response to constricting resources and changing landscape.
Accountability	Overall public disinterest in early care and education programs. Limited oversight or governance by funders or public. Strong resistance by early care and education field to externally driven results orientation and against loss of individual program autonomy through imposition of standards.	Growing expectations for public accountability. Increasing relationship between public financing and accountability for results. Mounting interest in creating governance and accountability systems. Movement toward defining performance through adherence to program and content standards and by measuring child outcomes, diminishing individuality across programs.
Relationship to K–12 education	Early educators suspicious of public schools and concerned that increased public school sponsorship of early care and education will eliminate existing community-based programs and promote developmentally inappropriate practice and content. Limited interest by public schools in early care and education—deemed outside the purview of K–12 education.	Public and charter schools increasingly providers of early care and education. Growing number of school districts with prekindergarten programs and/or fiscal relationship with community-based early care and education programs. Schools recognize early care and education as a means for promoting school readiness.

DESCRIPTORS OF THE EARLY CARE AND EDUCATION FIELD

Knowledge base	Knowledge base almost totally drawn from field of psychology. Practice reliant on theories of child development.	Growing expectations for early educators' knowledge base to include expertise in curriculum, instruction, and assessment as well as theories of child development.
Teacher qualifications	Teacher qualifications tied to sector and auspices, e.g., child care, public school, or Head Start. State child care regulations have primary responsibility for setting expectations for what teachers and administrators need to know and be able to do.	Movement toward 4-year degrees for teachers as prerequisite for working with prekindergarteners. Growing divide between teacher entry qualifications for child care and prekindergarten. Growing expectations for administrators to have management and leadership expertise.

Teacher role	Teachers as nurturers of "whole child," including physical, social, emotional, and intellectual development. "Teachers as nurturers" coexists with focus on caregivers as primarily responsible for ensuring child safety.	Shift to educational role with decreasing interest in teachers as nurturers. Teachers as instructors responsible for preparing children for success in school. Defining teacher role of interest primarily for those working with 3- and 4-year-olds.
Professional autonomy	Teacher-centered.	Decreased teacher autonomy. Teacher practice increasingly informed by state program, content, and early-learning standards—what children should know and be able to do.
Pedagogy	Continuum of practices that range from custodial care to facilitating development to didactic instruction. Developmentally appropriate practice codified by NAEYC.	Increasing public expectation for use of evidence-based practice and direct instruction.
Curriculum	Emergent curriculum based on children's interests. Reliance on play and child-selected activities as medium for implementing the curriculum.	Increasingly informed by state content and early-learning standards. Increased emphasis on literacy and numeracy skills. Growing presence of commercially packaged curricula. Many states identify acceptable curricula/curriculum models.

LEADERSHIP DIMENSIONS

Leadership demands	Field's small size and relative cohesion permit prominent individuals to function as "face" of early care and education.	Increasing quantity and complexity of issues placing greater demands on leaders. Increasingly difficult for single individual to speak on behalf of entire field. Limited institutional leadership capacity. Prominent change leadership often comes from individuals external to early care and education field.
Leadership needs	Program development primary focus. Emphasis on pedagogical leadership.	Call for differentiated leadership that can support systemic change and promote program quality: advocacy; pedagogical; administrative; community; conceptual.[a] Growing recognition of need for programmatic leadership capable of leading and managing organizations and ensuring their sustainability.
Leadership "pipeline"	Faculty in teacher preparation programs at colleges and universities primary source for new leaders.	Frequent concern expressed for meager number of emergent leaders. Systematic and/or field-wide leadership development opportunities largely nonexistent.

[a] Kagan & Newman, 1977.

63

Contra Costa Child Care Council
Learning Institute
1035 Detroit Ave. Suite 200
Concord, CA 94518

Characterizations of the Early Care and Education Field by Its Leaders

Between April 2005 and April 2006, we, as authors, conducted hour-long interviews with 40 individuals and hosted 4 focus groups with 14 people. The following five questions were posed to interviewees and focus group participants:

1. It's our sense that it's a new time for the early care and education field—that the field has entered into a transition period. What is your response to this notion? Can you identify specific transitions taking place?
2. In general, our observation of the field is that many diffuse activities are occurring with unknown impact; the field's fragmentation appears to be worsening—not improving. How do you respond to this observation?
3. What do you see as the conditions blocking the field's ability to create a collective vision that encompasses the field's multiple sectors and auspices?
4. What do you think the field is going to look like in 10 years? How different from your own view of what *should/could* happen is your idea of what *will* happen, thinking realistically?
5. Have you ever been involved in a change effort on the field's behalf? What was your experience?

Five cross-cutting themes about the field emerged from analyzing the responses to these questions:

- Its persona
- Its status

- Its leadership
- Its effectiveness as a change agent
- Its future

Interviewees' comments related to each of these five themes are provided below. These quotes come primarily from the interviews. A few quotes are included from focus group members or other participating colleagues. The quotes have been altered slightly in some instances in order to permit an embedded sentence to be understandable as a freestanding thought.

While the quantity of comments initially may seem overwhelming and the redundancy unnecessary, we chose for three reasons to err on the side of letting our interviewees' voices speak to you directly:

1. By presenting in the aggregate—for the first time—the viewpoints of a significant share of the field's leadership, we are exposing in a new way an assessment of the field's condition.
2. The unmistakable absence of a shared vision, the palpable resistance to change, and the apparent sense of impotence demonstrate the need for and importance of the field coming together to confront its adaptive challenges and envision a different future—and point to the potential consequences of failing to do so.
3. The responses underscore the pervasive impact on the field of the changing context outlined in Table A.1 (p. 60).

While some respondents spoke to a "glass half full," far more lamented the field's lack of focused movement toward a better future for children and for the early care and education field. The concern expressed for the field's well-being is sobering at best.

THE FIELD'S PERSONA

"Resistance to change is causing individual leaders within and external to the field to view the field as blocking positive change on behalf of children and families."

"We act like we own this field; we need to reach out to a broader public and give away some of the ownership."

"We have a sense of holy righteousness about children and, as a result, permit the perfect to be the enemy of the good."

"The field is so contentious, always, about its curriculum—a characteristic of the field."

"If there's one habit I'd like to break the field of, it's the knee-jerk reaction to change. We act as if 'the children' are ours alone, as if the bible of early childhood education was written in stone and never to be changed."

"We spend a lot of time and energy on reinforcing the wall of our fort against any new knowledge."

"We're all somewhat territorial. We say we're standing by principles, but the give-and-take is not there."

"There's so much siloed thinking; limited systemic thinking, consideration of the impact of what one is doing."

"Mistrust, differences of opinion are just so strong."

"We're so afraid of not being legitimate that we won't speak out."

"We desperately want to be recognized."

"For me, it's at a phase when I don't know where it's going. It's not organized. There's no leader. . . . I don't see the leaders now; the new people are not in a position to take over and dominate the field."

"I think the main issue is internalized depression. The work is so low status; we're totally desperate at some level. There's no trust. We're so anxious we protect what we have, even if it sucks."

"Because it's largely a woman's field, we don't want to deal with conflict."

"We don't have enough confidence to focus on moving forward."

"We have no united voice. Because we lost the window of opportunity [referring to mid-1990s], the focus has been on small ideas."

"We need to find commonality—find a more unified voice. We just fight, fight, fight. Otherwise we are going to be consumed by other professions."

"Folks can only see issues from their own perspectives. From my work on financing, I learned that folks completely saw financing from their own parochial view—from their place in the field."

"Out of scarcity, the field has a lot of competition: for who has right answers, for status and for resources."

"Our behavior makes us seem like whiners; makes us seem like we don't know what we want, especially to those outside the field."

"There's a culture in this field. If you go to meetings that bring folks together across organizations and listen as an alien, the culture is one of the problems."

"We are a field historically disenfranchised, underappreciated, and fearful of being overlooked."

"The slow pace has to do with the feeling of being second-class citizens, of not being chosen people. We believe our own hype, that anyone can do this work; we should welcome everyone. We have conflicting visions. We think the way to have diversity is to invite our neighbors in; it's a prejudicial way of looking at things. We're social workers to whole communities in a demeaning way."

THE FIELD'S STATUS

"The field is just getting tired."

"We are plagued with apathy and folks who are apolitical."

"I think the field's been in an ongoing evolution, and mission-driven folks have been on a quest to get something more sustainable."

"We've moved from a field more general and inclusive to something more disconnected. I'm unsure what it means to be a field. The worse-case scenario is that it's no longer a field—not unique."

"The field does not have any definition. One aspect of definition of a field is who is in it and who is out. Why is a 1st-grade teacher out and a neighbor who baby-sits in?"

"Pre-K has become aspirational and child care has become a necessary evil."

"We've lost the cohesion of care and education, of a field that integrates, of unifiers for the two elements. We're losing it conceptually, and it [the service] will exist only for a few."

"We are blending in with all the other systems, and no one will stand out."

"I like to know where I'm going. I usually do. I don't like the precariousness of the transition right now."

"I step in and out of the field. When I go back, it's as if I never left. People have a half-empty view. Things won't change without a shift in this regard."

"We are transitioning from fragmentation to systems despite digging in our heels for the status quo. This is what gives the impression of greater fragmentation. We are in a mode of greater turf protection, and we're not easily led to the table to be part of consensus building for a third party's idea."

"We spend our time fighting what's wrong versus what's right; we don't focus on what could be."

"Early childhood education has become politicized. All of the attention changes the context. Now that we're on the radar screen, there's more money but also more control."

"We're more networked and coordinated generally, but you have to look state by state."

"We are transitioning to bringing the pieces together."

"There is no vision or image of what early childhood education is."

"There are so many people in the field who lack education that the characteristics of the field are changing."

"I think to some extent that the degradation of the work force over the past 20 years means that the caliber of the field's rank and file is considerably less than it used to be."

"The field is not more fractured but more stuck in moving from here to there; there's not enough fresh thinking."

"We are fearful that our silos will be obliterated."

"The research has put the field into a tailspin as we reconcile 'care' and 'education,' cognitive skills and school readiness, emotionally healthy and socially competent. This splits us apart as if we have a major tsunami coming toward us."

"I worry about the shrinking professorate. We're not turning out new professionals who have a full sense of the whole child and the research relevant to the whole child. The field is still dominated by outdated teacher educators who are disconnected from the research and still focus only on social and emotional development."

"I'm anxious about identity with educational heritage. We're losing the developmental perspective and the traditions of family support and community development."

"It's a big elephant and everyone has a different part; there's no unifying factor."

"The hardest transition is the move from being on the fringe to becoming a mainstream issue. We're struggling to hold onto values and principles and still permit influential, powerful, sometimes overpowering folks to have influence."

"There's something of a vacuum in creating a new vision by powerful institutions and associations."

"No one is getting the big picture anymore."

"There's an institutionalization of the field in a way that's never happened before."

"Entities have legitimate concerns for self-protection; this applies to state organizations and providers; they're developing mechanisms to protect their boundaries. The worsening fragmentation is the fact that these boundaries are being crossed. The boundaries are being defended in more aggressive ways."

"Our fragmentation can, in part, be attributed to different philosophies on how we should work with children and families. This is good; it promotes debate. Some practices are appalling, but the movement is in the right direction."

"We may have reached a tipping point in size as an industry—of a size that can't be ignored. By way of evidence: the number of states doing economic impact studies, like in Vermont. The industry is bigger than timber and high-tech industries that Vermont spends money nurturing and supporting."

"We're heading toward something more common, with fewer distinctions among sectors, for example, length of day will be about being responsive to parents, but the purpose is still the same."

"I think we're coming to a commonality, toward being one large field, more common purpose."

"I think we're seeing decreased fragmentation because of efforts to have state pre-K and Head Start on the same page. In regards to child care, we see the use of quality-rating systems to make this happen. It's all pulling people in the direction of increased quality."

"There's a sense of new recognition, of new voices recognizing the importance of early childhood."

"Before, it was about auspices. Now added to the mix is public pre-K, and 0–3, and 4-year-olds. I guess fragmentation is worsening because there are more fragments."

"Veteran organizations are doing the work. Over the past 10 years, every 2 to 3 years, there are lots of smaller local groups who come and go, or who change leadership."

"There's a generational transition from the leaders, the luminaries, of the past 30 years."

"The field's passion can be a crutch. We're focused on children; so it's selfish to think about teachers, for example."

"I'd say that people are not organized in a way that has political clout, plus there's the impact on leadership of the absence of a deep infrastructure. It makes this work hard to do. There are folks who focus on the micropiece and others who take a systemic view, and there are not enough people to pull off the needed dialogues or to broker a common ground. There's lots of competing stuff and not enough force to pull it all together."

"The fragmentation that concerns me is the scrapping that we're doing among ourselves. We had made a lot of progress in seeing our various parts as part of a larger whole, but now we've gone back to scrapping among ourselves, of being territorial."

"Maybe early childhood education has been a step-child for so long it doesn't know how to be taken seriously—to be viewed as the 'good child'—and to take the next step. I see a self-imposed inferiority, fear of change, fighting one another."

"I don't know how committed the vast number of teachers are to the field. There's a 30% turnover of assistants; they're not viewing their work as careers. It's either a stepping-stone or a stopping place. I'm less sure about how much head teachers are committed, an impact of the fact that it's still viewed as an amateur's job."

"The field is being led rather than leading."

"We're going to be in an even larger mess if we don't focus."

"Because more is known, early educators need to know more. It's the harsh reality. What was good enough 10 years ago is not good enough now. We need to speak hard truths, to acknowledge that love of children is not enough."

THE FIELD'S LEADERSHIP

"We have leaders describing what should be done but very few showing how to move from what is to what should be."

"There is a lack of a common vision that we adhere to."

"What holds [you] back is the threat of petty stuff from inside that you have to put up with."

"The potential impact of our fragmentation is sabotage by members of the field. I do believe, though, that if people can see the light of increased stability, funding, and true career development, the field will see the benefit of a certain amount of consolidation."

"More and more is being discovered about brain development and learning. This knowledge has been used primarily for advocacy purposes rather than for shaping the field."

"I'm tired of separate entities. . . . Organization leaders and folks need to identify concrete things they can do together. We're squandering resources; we need collective advocacy; we need concrete goals for what we can do together."

"We're lacking really great leaders/scholars in higher education institutions."

"Individuals have difficulty making the necessary brutal choices that are needed."

"Leadership in national organizations needs to find common ground, concrete, doable action at a level higher than one organization's turf agenda."

"I sense that people are getting smarter in focusing on concrete, discrete strategies—on tackling parts of the puzzle—and that the field is more willing to accept this kind of strategy."

"As expressed by a legislator: You can't tell me what the two to three things are that you want to work on as a field, and then you blame others for encroaching on your territory; this won't work in the real world."

"We haven't been successful in including new stakeholders who can move issues. We haven't figured out how to work with stakeholders effectively and move the agenda."

"I think a lot of rhetoric about why people don't have to be qualified to work in the early childhood education field is very racist. It's posed as concern for community folk but in a country where you have to have credentials to make money, the only effect of not having credentials is limiting the mobility of people."

"If we got a big infusion of money, we probably wouldn't know how to use it."

"So many of the field's leaders are '60s kids; our kids are not enmeshed in that culture—so a different time."

"I rarely see agenda-setting documents anymore, and I don't think they exist. The work is mainly around practical implementation versus new design or vision."

"Are we more fragmented or drifting?"

"We are the most researched field with the least amount of doing."

"What stops the field from having a bigger vision? Small minds . . . hanging onto the past. No one takes on a new idea."

"I see older leaders anxious not to lose their power to younger leaders. Those 'behind us' are less prepared and not prepared to lead; there are no second lieutenants."

"People's egos get in the way—wanting [their] own piece to be recognized, competition for recognition and money. There's lots of female competition; it's ludicrous how leaders hold onto ego-driven ideas that if let go could open up the possibility of change."

"It's the same people saying the same things; they seem removed from what's happening in the field, especially the grass-roots practitioner."

"There's a lot to address; who's going to carry forward the mantle?"

"Like Democrats, we're all over the place. We don't stay on message. We have to learn to be inclusive and stay on message."

"Unifying strategies like common training, early-learning standards, and assessment are bringing us together."

"We have to focus on leadership development; we have mega capacity issues every which way you turn."

"We don't know how to make this [the changing landscape] work for us; it's a leadership issue."

"We have to have diverse leadership that looks like the field, including in higher education."

"New people [from outside the field] are the rock stars, and they're being recognized in ways that our long-standing leaders—who have held the field together—are not."

"We need to build a cadre to push the field in an outward direction. Presently we're at a standstill. Others will take our issue if we don't get on the same page."

"When it comes to getting more resources and new leadership vision, the field is not good at doing this. It's catalyzed from outside . . . blast from outside bringing the new way of thinking, the new resources it can use but can't develop for itself."

"We need to be more vocal; we're letting other people define us. As much as we want new voices, they're creating what we look like, and this scares me. It's one thing for economists to say pre-K works and saves dollars; it's something else for them to be defining a system. It's creating bad policy."

"Leaders outside of early childhood became the catalysts, and people inside the field began to scramble."

THE FIELD'S EFFECTIVENESS AS A CHANGE AGENT

"We aren't willing to go all the way with whatever sacrifices are necessary, with making a plan and following through. We stop and start and do not make a 100% commitment."

"The field needs to move from 'shaming for the right reasons' to identifying something winnable. This is a political game, and it's okay to sometimes be crass."

"I think we all want universal high-quality programs for children birth to 5. It has to be accomplished in phases. We need to stop fighting one another and focus on the big goal."

"We need a unifying movement and to organize as a political movement."

"Movements need great big thinkers. We don't have big ideas."

"Our internal tactics are holding us back. We have such low self-esteem and inferiority complex . . . whining . . . hand wringing . . . depressed . . . something bad is going to happen."

"We need to get political in a different kind of way—earlier. The political way now is outside of ourselves. We need to internally organize ourselves and externally find champions for state funding."

"The early care and education field has agreed to occupy a 'kid's ghetto'; we have to become a contender for resources so it's not babies against 4-year-olds but kids against the war in Iraq."

"Change won't happen without leadership of vision, of possibilities."

"We need a spark that revolutionizes the field to shift. The spark has to come from outside; we're so focused on our own navel we don't see what's going on."

"At the national level, it mostly seems like obstructionism to me. It seems caught up in partisan politics—folks not wanting any change."

"The status of actually working for kids hasn't changed but the status of engagement with the issue has. The field doesn't know how to deal with this. The field is being shut out; it's not unlike the fancy people moving into an older neighborhood."

"When we have the chance to change the conditions for the profession, we're fearful of who's going to be hurt, who will be left out, versus what's the issue and how do we want to tackle it."

"The field is so weak as a constituency that it can't prevent the political failures."

"There are different kinds of people involved in making a movement: people with knowledge of community, who can convene different kinds of people, who have a reputation for getting things done. The action in this country is coming from folks like Rob Reiner—not early childhood folks."

"What blocks us is not having a vision, creating a shared vision, having the ability to convene."

"People are not willing to grapple with the tough issues."

"Change is very regional, and there seems to be a shift in where the change is happening; we may be seeing a shift in regional leadership."

"We'll know that we're effective when a newly formed organization comes to combat the children's voice. They don't have to at this point."

"Where are the intellectual energy, the fortitude, and resources going to come from to think broadly and participate broadly, *and* not give up on the specialized area?"

THE FIELD'S FUTURE

"I don't have a sense of the field anymore, of what it means to be of this field."

"I don't know where the field will be in 10 years. What scares me about that is that I've always had a vision."

"There's a lot of potential because things are shaken up, resulting in deep conversations. How it will play itself out is anybody's guess."

"Increase in state pre-K; more emphasis on early education—not welfare; more attention to gaps in education."

"If you are an educationally successful person, early childhood is not a valid career option—it's bleak listening to me."

"There will be major losses in status, losses in organizations. To think that we would have a civil conversation is not realistic."

"It's a power struggle. The more powerful players may end up with even more influence."

"We will not be the people to make these decisions. Early childhood education is a public good. These are public policy decisions. We can inform them, but it's not just about today's young children; it's about the well-being of our country. So the decisions are not ours to make. . . . they come out of the political arena."

"I don't think it will be a national or state-by-state movement. It'll be done by convening the local community—by what people want for their own kids. The power in the U.S. is local communities. It's not going to be like Italy or France or the UK."

"The field is becoming an interdisciplinary set of people who touch children."

"I think it will become more difficult for small organizations with small budgets to rely on targeted support, to compete. Larger, more established nonprofits can invent, diversify, and cultivate donors."

"No doubt the field is becoming less fragmented. We pretend there weren't fragments; we're going toward one big field."

"We're moving to a P–16 structure. More and more state initiatives to support pre-K will result in continued fragmentation between very young and older children."

"We'll be a field, but we'll be smaller because of fragmentation."

"There's a long-term trend toward increased demand for quality; like private schools, that's where parental demand goes."

"Early childhood education will be a more education-driven model. What this adds up to is what third-party payers will support; they won't pay for care, but they'll pay for education."

"In 10 years, I suspect that we'll pretty much be in the same place."

"I would guess that we will have more universal pre-K for 4-year-olds; in the 10 most populous states, preschool will be an entitlement for all children or to a targeted population. And at the other end of the spectrum, parental leave will be available in three to five states. These states will, in turn, influence how other states respond to these issues."

"Aging leaders and their departure will have an impact on the field."

"It will soon clear that there will be differences between settings that are organized around outcomes for children versus convenience for parents."

APPENDIX C

Making Choices

Making choices about the early care and education field's purpose, identity, and responsibility involves decision making around the six-field defining questions outlined in Chapter 1. What follows are the decisions, with sample elements, that the field likely will want to consider so it can answer the field-defining questions. As suggested in Chapter 4, these questions can be used to raise awareness of the field's two adaptive challenges, and thereafter as part of the field's adaptive leadership work.

This appendix has three parts: decisions related to the issue of purpose, decisions related to the issue of identity, and decisions related to the issue of responsibility. These decision-making options are presented as *either–or* dichotomies in order to challenge us, as a field, to confront difficult alternatives. We know that forced selection does not acknowledge complexities, nuances, or the possibility for *both–and* responses; nor does dichotomous decision making conform to reality. Yet, at the beginning of our adaptive work, we believe that this discipline can help advance the field's deliberations. To this end, considering these alternatives in the context of group discussions that include people with diverse experiences and opinions will reveal more clearly the challenges and opportunities available to us as a field.

DECISIONS RELATED TO THE ISSUE OF PURPOSE—SAMPLE ELEMENTS

1A. The *primary* and *secondary* motives for the field's work should be:
(Choose one primary and one secondary response)
   a. Social and cultural competence
   b. Preparation for formal schooling
   c. Child development
   d. Early childhood education

  e. Protective, loving care
  f. Parental education
  g. Family support
  h. Parental employment
  i. Equal educational opportunity
  j. Social justice

1B. To what extent should program setting, ages of children served, and/or auspices inform the field's intent or purpose?

1C. To what extent—and how—should issues of race and class inform the field's intent or purpose?

2. The benefits of early care and education should be directed *primarily* to: (Choose one response)
  a. Children
  b. Families
  c. Community development
  d. Employers
  e. Societal policy priorities
   • economic self-sufficiency
   • criminal justice
   • school reform
   • community development

3. The chronological scope encompassed by early care and education should be: (Choose one response)
  a. Birth to 3 years
  b. Birth to the start of kindergarten
  c. Birth through kindergarten
  d. Birth through 8 years of age
  e. Birth through 8 years of age plus before- and after-school care
  f. Prekindergarten through grade 3

DECISIONS RELATED TO THE ISSUE OF IDENTITY—SAMPLE ELEMENTS

1. Early care and education as an occupation should be typified *primarily* by: (Choose one response)
  a. Love for children
  b. A developmental philosophy
  c. An educational philosophy
  d. State-established health and safety standards

2. Affiliation with the early care and education field should be determined mostly by: (Choose one response)
  a. Self-affiliation

    b. Years of experience working with children

    c. A recognized credential or degree achieved prior to entering the field

    d. A recognized credential or degree achieved after paid or unpaid experience working with children

    e. A credential or degree along with practicum/internship/experience completed prior to entering the field

    f. Competency-based performance

3. The field's core knowledge base should focus on: (Choose one response)

    a. Child development

    b. Curriculum and instruction

    c. Human ecology and family support

    d. Experiential knowledge of children

4. A formalized early care and education system should include: (Indicate all that should apply)

    a. License-exempt family, friend, and neighbor care

    b. Nanny care

    c. Nontraditional hour care (evenings/24-hour care)

    d. Regulated home-based care/family child care

    e. Center-based care and education

    f. School-based pre-K and kindergarten

    g. The primary grades

    h. Out-of-school time

5A. Early care and education should be organized as: (Choose one response)

    a. A single/unified field of endeavor

    b. A field comprising organized subfields

5B. If organized as a field comprising subfields, what should provide the organizing framework:

    a. The setting for early care and education

    b. The auspice for early care and education

    c. Segmented/specialized purposes

DECISIONS RELATED TO THE ISSUE OF RESPONSIBILITY—SAMPLE ELEMENTS

1. The early care and education field should be held accountable *primarily* to: (Rank-order the following categories)

    a. Children

    b. Families

    c. Private and public funders, including the state

   d. The general public
   e. The early care and education field's standard of efficacy
2. The early care and education field should hold itself responsible for:
   (Choose all that apply)
   a. Meeting established standards of program quality
   b. Ensuring children's basic health and safety
   c. Specified child outcomes
   d. Teacher performance
   e. Third-grade achievement test scores
3. With respect to comprehensive services (such as parental education
   and physical and oral health services), the early care and education
   field should: (Choose one response)
   a. Have no direct responsibility
   b. Serve as a resource to families
   c. Actively coordinate comprehensive services at the program level
   d. Ensure comprehensive services are coordinated at a broader
      state/local policy level
4. Changes in the early care and education field should be determined
   primarily by: (Choose one response)
   a. States
   b. The federal government
   c. Individuals affiliated with early care and education
   d. Parents
   e. Tax payers

Based on your responses to decisions related to purpose, identity, and responsibility, what should be the field's nonnegotiable features?

Notes

INTRODUCTION

1. The trademarked phrase is used with permission of the National Association for the Education of Young Children.
2. Heifetz, 1994; Heifetz & Laurie, 1999; Heifetz & Linsky, 2002.
3. Senge & Kaufer, n.d.
4. Use of the term *early childhood field* in this way aligns with Bruner's use of the term *early learning system*, which he describes as a system of systems encompassing early care and education plus related systems. Bruner, 2004.
5. We are uncertain whom to credit for coining this phrase.
6. Wheatley, 1992, p. 48.
7. See Dreeben, 2005; Johnson, 2005; Morgan, 2006; Sykes, 1987.
8. S.L. Carter, 1996, p. 7.

CHAPTER 1

1. Beatty, 1995; Michel, 1999; Snyder, 1972; Zigler & Muenchow, 1992.
2. Barnett, Hustedt, Robin, & Schulman, 2003; Kauerz, 2006; "Pre-K Education," 2005.
3. See, for example, Bruner, 2004; Cauthen, Knitzer, & Ripple, 2000; Morgan & Costley, 2004.
4. See, for example, Kagan & Scott-Little, 2004; Morgan & Helburn, 2006.
5. Morgan & Helburn, 2006, p. 11.
6. Goffin, 2001; Goffin & Wilson, 2001a; Lee & Walsh, 2005; Snyder, 1972; Swadener & Kessler, 1991.
7. Kagan & Cohen, 1997.
8. Kagan & Cohen, 1997; Kagan & Rigby, 2003.
9. Folbre, 1994; Lynch, 2004.
10. For example, Rodd, 1994; Talan & Bloom, 2004.
11. Kagan & Neuman, 1997.

12. Kagan & Bowman, 1997a.

13. See, for example, Committee for Economic Development, 2004; Heckman, 2006b; Lynch, 2004; Rolnick & Grunewald, 2003.

14. Hamel & Prahalad, 1994, p. x.

15. As noted in the Acknowledgments, interviews, focus groups, and structured interactions informed our understanding of the present state of early care and education. The insights of these leaders are woven throughout, even if not always directly acknowledged. See also "Exchange Every Day," 2005.

16. In the absence of a shared, field-wide answer to this question, we recognize that every time the phrase "early care and education field" is used, we cannot count on it conveying shared meaning.

17. Caldwell, 1967, p. 348. The first author has raised a variation of this question on two previous occasions as well; see Goffin, 1996, 2001.

18. Smith, 1987, p. 38, emphasis in original.

19. Heifetz & Laurie, 1999, p. 73.

20. Snyder, 1972.

21. Kagan & Bowman, 1997a, p. 157, emphasis added.

22. Heifetz, 1994; Heifetz & Laurie, 1999; Heifetz & Linsky, 2002.

23. Heifetz, 1994.

24. This approach to discussing occupations is taken from Dreeben, 2005.

25. Caldwell, 2004; *Early Childhood Care,* 2002; What's in a name?, 2001.

26. Kagan & Bowman, 1997b, p. 6.

27. Early et al., 2005; Helburn, 1995.

28. For example, see Gilliam, & Marchesseault, 2005; Marshall, Dennehy, Johnson-Staub, & Robeson, 2005.

29. Carnegie Corporation of New York, 1994; National Research Council, 2001; National Research Council and Institute of Medicine, 2000.

30. Snyder, 1972, p. 71.

31. Snyder, 1972, p. 182.

32. Bredekamp, 1987; Goffin & Wilson, 2001b.

33. Kagan, 1991, p. xi.

34. National Institute for Early Childhood Professional Development, 1993.

35. Kagan & Cohen, 1996, 1997.

36. Kagan & Cohen, 1997; Kagan & Rigby, 2003.

37. Cohen, 2001.

38. "Stepping up Together," 1999.

39. Gallagher, Clifford, & Maxwell, 2004, p. 34.

40. Bredekamp & Copple, 1997.

41. Hamel & Prahalad, 1994, p. xi.

42. Takanishi, 2004.

CHAPTER 2

1. Herzenberg, Price, & Bradley, 2005.

2. For the most recent economic impact studies, go to the National Economic

Development and Law Center website (www.nedlc.org). See also Committee for Economic Development, 2006; Heckman, 2006a, 2006b; Lynch, 2004; Rolnick & Grunewald, 2003.

    3. Neugebauer, 2006.

    4. Graves, 2005; Kauerz, 2006.

    5. Ackerman, Barnett, & Robin, 2005; AFT and CCW/AFTEF, CCSSO, ECS, NAESP, NEA and NAEYC, 2005; Gullo, 2006; Howard, 2006b; Kauerz, 2005.

    6. America 2000: An Education Strategy, 1991.

    7. Carnegie Corporation of New York, 1994; Shore, 1997; "Your Child Birth to Three," 2000; "Your Child from Birth to Three," 1997.

    8. Carnegie Corporation of New York, 1994; National Research Council, 2001; National Research Council and Institute of Medicine, 2000.

    9. Campbell, Ramey, Pungello, Sparling, & Miller-Johnson, 2002; "Fight Crime," 2004; Reynolds, 2000; Schweinhart, 2004; Schweinhart, Barnes, & Weikart, 1993.

    10. Committee for Economic Development, 2004; Council of Chief State School Officers, 1999; Heckman, 2006a, 2006b; Karoly, Kilburn, & Cannon, 2005; Lynch, 2004; National Association of Elementary School Principals, 2005; Rolnick & Grunewald, 2003.

    11. See, for example, Goffin & Wilson, 2001a; Grubb & Lazerson, 1988; Lazerson, 1971, 1972; Michel, 1999; Pizzo, 1983.

    12. Barnett, Hustedt, Robin, & Schulman, 2005; see also Committee for Economic Development at www.ced.com for additional examples.

    13. By way of example, see Schumacher & Lombardi, 2003; Scott-Little, Kagan, & Frelow, 2003; see also www.buildinitiative.org for a sampling of state system development efforts.

    14. Clifford, 2005, p. 4.

    15. Drucker, 1989/2003, p. ix, emphasis in original.

    16. Hymes, 1991; Kagan & Zigler, 1987; Mitchell & Modigliani, 1989; Mitchell, Seligson, & Marx, 1987.

    17. Biber, 1969.

    18. Schwartz, 2003, p. 223.

    19. Zander & Zander, 2000.

    20. Early et al., 2005; also see Christina & Nicholson-Goodman, 2005; "Pre-K Education," 2005.

    21. See, for example, Campbell, Entmacher, Matsui, Firvida, & Love, 2006; Chalfie & Campbell, 2005.

    22. Howard, 2006a; Leadership Matters, 2006.

    23. Brooks, 2006; Dionne, 2006.

    24. See, for example, Kagan & Scott-Little, 2004; Scott-Little, Kagan, & Frelow, 2006.

    25. See, for example, "Is All-Day Kindergarten Worth It?," 2006; Paulson, 2006; "Rob Reiner Takes Leave," 2006.

    26. Barnett, 1996; "Fight Crime," 2004; Karoly, Kilburn, & Cannon, 2005; Schweinhart, 2004.

    27. Rhode Island KIDS COUNT, 2005.

28. See, for example, Goffin & Wilson, 2001a.

29. Scott-Little, Kagan, & Frelow, 2006.

30. This statement is from Harriet Egertson and quoted, with permission from the author, from the National Association of Early Childhood Specialists in State Departments of Education list-serv on March 21, 2006.

31. For a contrary viewpoint, see Lee & Walsh, 2005.

32. Christina & Nicholson-Goodman, 2005; Early et al., 2006.

33. Howard, 2006b; Kagan & Kauerz, 2006.

34. Morgan & Helburn, 2006.

35. Morgan & Helburn, 2006, p. 12.

36. Bailey, Oyemade, Waxler, & Washington, 2006; Oyemade, Washington, & Gullo, 1989; Slaughter, Washington, Oyemade, & Lindsey, 1988; Washington & Oyemade, 1995; Zigler & Muenchow, 1992.

37. Currie, 2001; Haskins, 2004; Haskins & Sawhill, 2003; U.S. General Accounting Office, 1998.

38. Kagan & Neuman, 1997, p. 59.

39. Drucker, 1989/2003, p. 149.

40. See, for example, Collins, 2005; Schein, 2004; Senge, 1990; Senge & Kaufer, n.d.

41. Public Agenda, 2000, p. 11.

42. Collins, 2005, p. 5.

43. Drucker, 1989/2003, p. xiii.

CHAPTER 3

1. Clifford, 1998, p. 2.

2. Schein, 2004.

3. See Morgan, 1998.

4. Katz, personal communication, July 10, 2005.

5. Schwartz, 2003, p. 4.

6. Smith, 1987, p. 38.

7. Temporary Assistance for Needy Families (TANF) is a block grant created by the Personal Responsibility and Work Opportunity Reconciliation Act of 1996, as part of a federal effort to "end welfare as we know it." The TANF block grant replaced the Aid to Families with Dependent Children program, which had provided cash welfare to poor families with children since 1935. Commonly known as welfare, TANF requires adult recipients with a child over age 1 to participate in a work activity with the intent of helping recipients gain the experience needed to become economically self-sufficient. In this regard, the policy specifically provides assistance to needy families so that children may be cared for in their own homes or in the homes of relatives. For a recent study of the impact of this policy in one state, see Washington, Marshall, Robinson, Modigliani, & Rosa, 2006.

8. Whitebook, 2002.

9. Kontos, Howes, Shinn, & Galinsky, 1995; Loeb, Fuller, Kagan, & Carrol, 2004.

10. Child Mental Health Foundations and Agencies Network, 2000; National Research Council and Institute of Medicine, 2000; Raver, 2002; Set for Success, 2002.

11. Morgan & Helburn, 2006, p. 10.

12. For example, see Covey, 1994; Senge, 1990.

13. Erikson, 1963, p. 261.

14. Erikson, 1963.

15. National Association for the Education of Young Children, n.d.

16. American Nurses Association, n.d.

17. National Association of Social Workers, n.d.

18. Dreeben, 2005.

19. Bowman, 2001.

20. Bowman, 2001, p. 176.

21. See, for example, Saluja, Early, & Clifford, 2002; Whitebook, Sakai, Gerber, & Howes, 2001.

22. Helburn, 1995; Early, Barbarin, Bryant, Burchinal, Chang, Clifford, et al., 2005.

23. Dreeben, 2005, p. 52.

24. Dreeben, 2005, p. 52.

25. Barnett, 2004; National Research Council, 2001; Whitebook, 2003.

26. A mandate in the 1998 Head Start Act required that by September 30, 2003, at least half of all Head Start teachers in center-based programs must have an associate, baccalaureate, or advanced degree in early childhood education or a degree in a related field, with preschool teaching experience. For current requirements, see Head Start Program Performance Standards and Other Regulations (U.S. Department of Health and Human Services, Administration for Children and Families, Office of Head Start, n.d.).

27. Costrell, 2006; Lamy, Barnett, & Jung, 2005.

28. Gilliam & Marchesseault, 2005; Morgan et al., 1993.

29. Goffin & Wilson, 2001a.

30. Hatch et al., 2002; Tobin, 1992.

31. Bevilacqua, 1997, p. 1.

32. Bevilacqua, 1997; Dickinson, 2002; Hatch et al., 2002; Johnson & Johnson, 1992; Lee & Walsh, 2005; Mallory & New, 1994; Swadener & Kessler, 1991.

33. Goffin & Wilson, 2001b.

34. Bowman, 2001, p. 177.

35. Marcon, 1992, 1999, 2002; Montie, Xiang, & Schweinhart, 2006; Schweinhart, 2004; Schweinhart & Weikart, 1997.

36. See, for example, NAEYC Early Childhood Program Standards and Accreditation Criteria, 2005.

37. Early et al., 2005; Helburn, 1995.

38. M. Carter, 2006, p. 32.

39. Morgan & Costley, 2004.

40. Barnett, 1996; "Fight Crime," 2004; Karoly, Kilburn, & Cannon, 2005; Schweinhart, 2004.

41. Morgan & Helburn, 2006; Washington, Ferris, Hughes, Scott-Chandler, Luk, & Bates, 2006.

42. McDaniel, Issac, Brooks, & Hatch, 2005; National Association for the Education of Young Children, 2004; National Association of State Boards of Education, 2001; Steinberg, 2002.

43. Scott-Little, Kagan, & Frelow, 2003, 2006.

44. U.S. Department of Health and Human Services, Administration for Children and Families, Office of Head Start, n.d.

45. National Association for the Education of Young Children, 2005.

46. Early et al., 2005; Helburn, 1995.

47. Herzenberg, Price, & Bradley, 2005.

48. School readiness, 2005.

CHAPTER 4

1. Heifetz, 1994; Heifetz & Linsky, 2002; Heifetz, Kania, & Kramer, 2004; Heifetz & Laurie, 1999.

2. Heifetz, 1994, p. 24.

3. Heifetz, 1994, p. 22.

4. Heifetz, 1994.

5. Heifetz, Kania, & Kramer, 2004, p. 23.

6. Heifetz, 1994; Heifetz, Kania, & Kramer, 2004; Senge et al., 1999.

7. Heifetz, 1994; Heifetz & Laurie, 1999.

8. Senge, 1999, p. 16.

9. Heifetz, 1994; Heifetz, Kania, & Kramer, 2004.

10. Senge, 1999.

11. Krajec, Bloom, Talen, & Clark, 2001; Saluja, Early, & Clifford, 2002; Whitebook, 2002; Whitebook, Sakai, Gerber, & Howes, 2001.

12. Whitebook, 2002; Whitebook & Phillips, 1999.

13. Blackwell, 2003; Washington, 2005.

14. By way of two examples: (1) In its move toward universal prekindergarten, Massachusetts appointed an all-White board for its new Department of Early Care and Education; the commissioner and all senior staff also are White. (2) In one of our focus groups, a national leader expressed total unawareness of the presence of race and class overtones in debates on different strategies for promoting universal prekindergarten education.

15. Washington & Andrews, 1998.

16. Mayo & Nohria, 2005.

17. Heifetz, 1994; Mathews & McAfee, 1997.

18. Heifetz, 1994; Heifetz, Kania, & Kramer, 2004; Senge et al., 1999.

19. Heifetz, 1994; Kotter, 1995.

20. Heifetz, 1994; Heifetz, Kania, & Kramer, 2004.

References

Ackerman, D. J., Barnett, W. S., & Robin, K. B. (2005). *Making the most of kindergarten: Present trends and future issues in the provision of full-day kindergarten.* Retrieved March 30, 2006, from http://nieer.org/resources/policyreports/report4.pdf

AFT and CCW/AFTEF, CCSSO, ECS, NAESP, NEA and NAEYC. (2005). Why we care about the K in K–12. *Young Children, 60*(2), 54–56.

America 2000: An education strategy. (1991). Washington, DC: U.S. Department of Education.

American Nurses Association. (n.d.). Membership application: Join ANA membership. Retrieved February 22, 2006, from https://nursingworld.org/memapp/index.cfm

Bailey, U., Oyemade, J., Waxler, T., & Washington, V. (2006). Head Start: Translating research into policy and practice. In D. Slaughter-Defoe, A. M. Garrett, & A. O. Harrison-Hale (Eds.), *Our children too: A history of the black caucus of the Society for Research in Child Development, 1973–1997* (pp. 145–161). Boston: Blackwell.

Barnett, W. S. (1996). *Lives in the balance: Age-27 benefit–cost analysis of the High/Scope Perry Preschool program.* Ypsilanti, MI: High/Scope Educational Research Foundation.

Barnett, W. S. (2004). *Better teachers, better preschools: Student achievement linked to teacher qualifications* (Issue 2). Retrieved November 15, 2005, from http://nieer.org/resources/policybriefs/2.pdf

Barnett, W. S., Hustedt, J. T., Robin, K. B., & Schulman, K. L. (2003). *The state of preschool: 2003 state preschool yearbook.* New Brunswick, NJ: National Institute for Early Education Research, Rutgers University.

Barnett, W. S., Hustedt, J. T., Robin, K. B., & Schulman, K. L. (2005). *The state of preschool: 2005 state preschool yearbook.* New Brunswick, NJ: National Institute for Early Education Research, Rutgers University.

Beatty, B. (1995). *Preschool education in America: The culture of young children from the colonial era to the present.* New Haven, CT: Yale University Press.

Bevilacqua, L. (1997, Winter/Spring). Ten years later: Developmentally appropriate practice: What have we learned? *Common Knowledge, 10*(1/2). Retrieved

March 15, 2006, from http://coreknowledge.org/CK/about/print/DevAppPrac .htm

Biber, B. (1969). Challenges ahead for early childhood education. *Young Children,* 24(4), 196–205.

Blackwell, A. G. (2003). Preface. In D. S. Marsh, M. Hawk, & K. Putnam (Eds.), *Leadership for policy change: Strengthening communities of color through leadership development.* Washington, DC: PolicyLink. Retrieved March 30, 2006, from www.policylink.org/pdfs/LeadershipForPolicyChange.pdf

Bowman, B. T. (2001). Facing the future. In *NAEYC at 75: Reflections on the past, challenges for the future* (pp. 167–182). Washington, DC: National Association for the Education of Young Children.

Bowman, B. T., & Kagan, S. L. (1997). Moving the leadership agenda. In S. L. Kagan & B. T. Bowman (Eds.), *Leadership in early care and education* (pp. 157–160). Washington, DC: National Association for the Education of Young Children.

Bredekamp, S. (Ed.). (1987). *Developmentally appropriate practice in early childhood programs serving children from birth through age 8* (Exp. ed.). Washington, DC: National Association for the Education of Young Children.

Bredekamp, S., & Copple, C. (Eds.). (1997). *Developmentally appropriate practice in early childhood programs* (Rev. ed.). Washington, DC: National Association for the Education of Young Children.

Brooks, D. (2006, June 4). Good intentions, bad policy. *New York Times,* p. 14.

Bruner, C. (with Wright, M. S., Gebhard, B., & Hibbard, S.). (2004). *Building an early learning system: The ABCs of planning and governance structures.* Des Moines, IA: State Early Childhood Policy Technical Assistance Network in collaboration with the Build Initiative.

Caldwell, B. M. (1967). On reformulating the concept of early childhood education—Some whys needing wherefores. *Young Children,* 22(6), 48–56.

Caldwell, B. M. (2004). *What's in a name?* Retrieved March 16, 2004, from https://secure.ccie.com/resources/view_article.php?file=caldwell_name

Campbell, F. A., Ramey, C. T., Pungello, E. P., Sparling, J., & Miller-Johnson, S. (2002). Early childhood education: Young adult outcomes from the Abecedarian Project. *Applied Developmental Science,* 6(1), 42–47.

Campbell, N. D., Entmacher, J., Matsui, A. K., Firvida, C. M., & Love, C. (2006). *Making child care less taxing: Improving state child and dependent care provisions.* Retrieved March 1, 2006, from http://www.nwlc.org/pdf/MakingCareLess Taxing2006.pdf

Carnegie Corporation of New York. (1994). *Starting points: Meeting the needs of our youngest children.* New York: Author.

Carter, M. (2006, May/June). Standards or standardization: Where are we going? *Exchange,* No. 169, pp. 32–36.

Carter, S. L. (1996). *Integrity.* New York: Basic Books.

Cauthen, N. K., Knitzer, J., & Ripple, C. (2000). *Map and track: State initiatives for young children and families.* New York: National Center for Children in Poverty.

Chalfie, D., & Campbell, N. D. (2005). *Power to the people: The effectiveness of ballot measures in advancing early care and education.* Retrieved January 21, 2006, from http://www.nwlc.org/pdf/PowertothePeopleFinal2005.pdf

Child Mental Health Foundations and Agencies Network. (2000). *A good beginning: Sending America's children to school with the social and emotional competence they need to succeed.* Bethesda, MD: National Institute of Mental Health.

Christina, R., & Nicholson-Goodman, J. (2005). *Going to scale with high-quality early education: Choices and consequences in universal pre-kindergarten efforts* (Tech. Rep.). Santa Monica, CA: RAND Corporation. Retrieved September 17, 2005, from http://www.rand.org/pubs/technical_reports/TR237/

Clifford, R. M. (1998). Beyond parallel play. *Young Children, 53*(1), 2, 19.

Clifford, R. M. (2005, Fall). Intervention studies then and now. *Early Developments, 9*(2), 4–5.

Cohen, S. (2001). *Championing child care.* New York: Columbia University Press.

Collins, J. (2005). *Good to great and the social sectors: A monograph to accompany Good to Great.* Boulder, CO: Author.

Committee for Economic Development. (2004). *A new framework for assessing the benefits of early education* (Working paper). Retrieved October 15, 2005, from http://www.ced.org/docs/report/report_preschool_2004_assessingbenefits.pdf

Committee for Economic Development. (2006). *The economic promise of investing in high quality preschool: Using early education to improve economic growth and the fiscal sustainability of the states and the nation.* Washington, DC: Author. Retrieved May 10, 2006, from http://www.ced.org/docs/report/report_prek_econpromise.pdf

Costrell, R. M. (2006). *Massachusetts' Hancock case and the adequacy doctrine.* Cambridge, MA: Rappaport Institute of Greater Boston, Harvard University.

Council of Chief State School Officers. (1999). *Early childhood and family education: New realities, new opportunities* (A Council Policy Statement). Washington, DC: Author.

Covey, S. R. (1994). *First things first.* New York: Simon & Schuster.

Currie, J. (2001 March). *A fresh start for Head Start* (Children's Roundtable Report No. 5). Washington, DC: Brookings Institute.

Dickinson, D. (2002). Shifting images of developmentally appropriate practice as seen through different lenses. *Educational Researcher, 31*(1), 26–32.

Dionne, E. J. (2006, June 9). Lessons for liberals in California. *The Washington Post,* p. A23.

Dreeben, R. (2005). Teaching and the competence of organizations. In L. V. Hedges & B. Schneider (Eds.), *The social organization of schooling* (pp. 51–71). New York: Russell Sage Foundation.

Drucker, P. F. (2003). *The new realities.* New Brunswick, NJ: Transaction. (Original work published 1989)

Early, D., Barbarin, O., Bryant, D., Burchinal, M., Chang, F., Clifford, R., et al. (2005, May 24). *Pre-kindergarten in eleven states: NCEDL's multi-state study of pre-kindergarten & study of state-wide early education programs (SWEEP)— Preliminary descriptive report* (NCEDL working paper). Retrieved June 30, 2005, from http://www.fpg.unc.edu/~ncedl/pdfs/SWEEP_MS_summary_final.pdf

Early, D. M., Bryant, D. M., Pianta, R. C., Clifford, R. M., Burchinal, M. R., Ritchie, et al. (2006). Are teachers' education, major, and credentials related to classroom quality and children's academic gains in pre-kindergarten? *Early Child-hood Research Quarterly, 21,* 174–195.

Early childhood care? Development? Education? (2002, March). UNESCO Policy Brief on Early Childhood. Retrieved June 20, 2002, from http://unesdoc.unesco.org/images/0013/001373/137337e.pdf

Erikson, E. H. (1963). *Childhood and society* (2nd ed.). New York: Norton.

Exchange every day. (2005). Interview with Gwen Morgan. Retrieved October 5, 2005, from http://www.childcareexchange.com/eed/issue.php?id=1286

Fight crime invest in kids. (2004). *Quality pre-kindergarten key to crime prevention and school success* (Research Brief). Washington, DC: Author. Retrieved July 10, 2006, from www.fightcrime.org.

Folbre, N. (1994). Children as public goods: The economic support of child-raising. *AEA Papers and Proceedings, 84*(2), 86–90.

Gallagher, J. J., Clifford, R. M., & Maxwell, K. (2004, September 9–10). *Getting from here to there: Organization and coordination of early childhood services.* For Conference on Creating a National Plan for the Education of 4 Year Olds, sponsored by the Brookings Institute and the National Prekindergarten Center at UNC at Chapel Hill.

Gilliam, W. S., & Marchesseault, C. M. (2005). *From capitols to classrooms, policies to practice: State-funded prekindergarten at the classroom level: Part I. Who's teaching our youngest students? Teacher education and training, experience, compensation and benefits, and assistant teachers.* New Haven, CT: Yale University Child Study Center. Retrieved March 1, 2006, from nieer.org/resources/files/NPSteachers.pdf

Goffin, S. G. (1996). Child development: Knowledge and early childhood teacher preparation: Assessing the relationship—A special collection. *Early Childhood Research Quarterly, 11,* 117–133.

Goffin, S. G. (2001). Whither early childhood care and education in the next century? In L. Corno (Ed.), *Education across a century: The centennial volume* (pp. 140–163). One Hundreth Yearbook of the National Society for the Study of Education, Part 1. Chicago: National Society for the Study of Education.

Goffin, S. G., & Wilson, C. (2001a). *Curriculum models and early childhood education: Appraising the relationship* (2nd ed.). Upper Saddle River, NJ: Merrill Prentice Hall.

Goffin, S. G., & Wilson, C. S. (2001b). The developmental-interaction approach. In *Curriculum models and early childhood education: Appraising the relationship* (2nd ed., pp. 65–95). Columbus, OH: Merrill Prentice Hall.

Graves, B. (2005). *Getting there: PK–3 as public education's base camp.* New York: Foundation for Child Development.

Grubb, W. N., & Lazerson, M. (1988). *Broken promises: How Americans fail their children.* Chicago: University of Chicago Press.

Gullo, D. F. (Ed.). (2006). *Kindergarten today: Teaching and learning in the kindergarten year.* Washington, DC: National Association for the Education of Young Children.

Hamel, G., & Prahalad, C. K. (1994). *Competing for the future.* Boston: Harvard Business School Press.

Haskins, R. (2004, Winter). Competing visions. *Education Next*, pp. 27–33. Retrieved September 22, 2005, from http://www.brookings.edu/views/articles/haskins/20040219.htm

Haskins, R., & Sawhill, I. (2003, July). *The future of Head Start* (Welfare Reform and Beyond, Policy Brief No. 27). Washington DC: Brookings Institute.

Hatch, A., Bowman, B., Jor'dan, J., Morgan, C. L., Hart, C., Soto, L. D., et al. (2002). Developmentally appropriate practice: Continuing the dialogue. *Contemporary Issues in Early Childhood, 3*(3), 439–457.

Heckman, J. J. (2006a, January 10). Catch 'em young [Editorial]. *Wall Street Journal*, p. A14.

Heckman, J. J. (2006b, January 10). *Investing in disadvantaged young children is an economically efficient policy.* Paper presented at CED/Pew Charitable Trusts/PNC Financial Services Group Forum on Building the Economic Case for Investment in Preschool, New York.

Heifetz, R. A. (1994). *Leadership without easy answers.* Cambridge, MA: Belknap Press of Harvard University Press.

Heifetz, R. A., Kania, J. V., & Kramer, M. R. (2004, Winter). Leading boldly: Foundations can move past traditional approaches to create social change through imaginative—and even controversial—leadership. *Stanford Social Innovation Review, 23*, 21–31. Retrieved May 10, 2006, from http://www.ssireview.org/articles/entry/leading_boldly/

Heifetz, R. A., & Laurie, D. L. (1999). Mobilizing adaptive work: Beyond visionary leadership. In J. A. Conger, G. M. Spreitzer, & E. E. Lawler, III (Eds.), *The leader's change handbook: An essential guide to setting direction and taking action* (pp. 55–86). San Francisco: Jossey-Bass.

Heifetz, R. A., & Linsky, M. (2002). *Leadership on the line: Staying alive through the dangers of leading.* Boston: Harvard Business School Press.

Helburn, S. W. (Ed.). (1995). *Cost, quality, and child outcomes in child care centers* (Tech. Rep.). Denver: Department of Economics, Center for Research in Economics and Social Policy, University of Colorado at Denver.

Herzenberg, S., Price, M., & Bradley, D. (2005). *Losing ground in early childhood education: Declining workforce qualifications in an expanding industry.* Washington, DC: Economic Policy Institute.

Howard, M. (2006a). *Current and emerging state policy trends in early childhood education: A review of governors' 2006 state of the state addresses* (Policy Brief). Retrieved April 1, 2006, from http://www.ecs.org/clearinghouse/68/21/6821.pdf

Howard, M. (2006b). *Emerging issues 2006* (Policy Brief). Denver, CO: Education Commission of the States. Retrieved June 1, 2006, from http://www.ecs.org/clearinghouse/68/84/6884.pdf

Hymes, J. (1991). *Early childhood education. Twenty years in review: A look at 1971–1990.* Washington, DC: National Association for the Education of Young Children.

Is all-day kindergarten worth it? (2006). *Cincinnati Enquirer.* Retrieved March 14, 2006, from http://m01.webmail.aol.com/15106/aol/en-us/Mail/display-message.aspx

Johnson, F., & Johnson, K. M. (1992). Clarifying the developmental perspective in response to Carta, Schwartz, Atwater and McConnell. *Topics in Early Childhood Special Education, 12,* 439–457.

Johnson, S. M. (2005). The prospects for teaching as a profession. In L. V. Hedges & B. Schneider (Eds.), *The social organization of schooling* (pp. 72–90). New York: Russell Sage Foundation.

Kagan, S. L. (1991). Editor's preface. In S. L. Kagan (Ed.), *The care and education of America's young children: Obstacles and opportunities* (pp. ix–xiii). Ninetieth yearbook of the National Society for the Study of Education, Part I. Chicago: National Society for the Study of Education.

Kagan, S. L., & Bowman, B. T. (Eds.). (1997a). *Leadership in early care and education.* Washington, DC: National Association for the Education of Young Children.

Kagan, S. L., & Bowman, B. T. (1997b). Leadership in early care and education: Issues and challenges. In S. L. Kagan & B. T. Bowman (Eds.), *Leadership in early care and education* (pp. 3–8). Washington, DC: National Association for the Education of Young Children.

Kagan, S. L., & Cohen, N. E. (Eds.). (1996). *Reinventing early care and education: A vision for a quality system.* San Francisco: Jossey-Bass.

Kagan, S. L., & Cohen, N. E. (1997). *Not by chance: Creating an early care and education system for America's children* [Full report]. The Quality 2000 Initiative. New Haven, CT: Bush Center in Child Development and Social Policy.

Kagan, S. L., & Kauerz, K. (2006, January). *Early childhood school readiness in Ohio: Governance and accountability* (System Design Work Group Papers). Commissioned by the School Readiness Solutions Group. Columbus: Ohio Department of Education.

Kagan, S. L., & Neuman, M. J. (1997). Conceptual leadership. In S. L. Kagan & B. T. Bowman (Eds.), *Leadership in early care and education* (pp. 59–64). Washington, DC: National Association for the Education of Young Children.

Kagan, S. L., & Rigby, E. (2003). *Policy matters: Setting and measuring benchmarks for state policies.* Washington, DC: Center for the Study of Social Policy.

Kagan, S. L., & Scott-Little, C. (2004). Early learning standards: Changing the parlance and practice of early childhood education? *Phi Delta Kappan, 85*(5), 388–396.

Kagan, S. L., & Zigler, E. F. (Eds.). (1987). *Early schooling: The national debate.* New Haven, CT: Yale University Press.

Karoly, L. A., Kilburn, M. R., & Cannon, J. S. (2005). *Early childhood interventions: Proven results, future promise.* Santa Monica, CA: RAND Corporation.

Kauerz, K. (2005). *Full day kindergarten: A study of state policies in the United States.* Denver, CO: Education Commission of the States.

Kauerz, K. (2006). *Ladders of learning: Fighting fade-out by advancing PK–3 alignment* (Issue Brief). Washington, DC: New America Foundation.

Kontos, S., Howes, C., Shinn, M., & Galinsky, E. (1995). *Quality in family child care and relative care.* New York: Teachers College Press.

Kotter, J. P. (1995). Leading change. Why transformation efforts fail. *Harvard Business Review, 73*(3), 59–67.

Krajec, V., Bloom, P., Talen, T., & Clark, D. (2001). *Who's caring for the kids? Status of the early childhood workforce in Illinois.* Wheeling, IL: McCormick Tribune Center for Early Childhood Leadership.

Lamy, C., Barnett, W. S., & Jung, K. (2005). *The effects of New Jersey's Abbott Preschool program on young children's school readiness.* New Brunswick, NJ: National Institute for Early Education Research, Rutgers University.

Lazerson, M. (1971). Social reform and early childhood education: Some historical perspectives. In R. H. Anderson & H. G. Shane (Eds.), *As the twig is bent* (pp. 22–33). Boston: Houghton Mifflin.

Lazerson, M. (1972). The historical antecedents of early childhood education. In I. J. Gordon & H. G. Richey (Eds.), *Early childhood education* (pp. 33–53). Seventy-first Yearbook of the National Society for the Study of Education, Part 2. Chicago: National Society for the Study of Education.

Leadership matters: Governors' pre-K proposals. (2006). Retrieved June 15, 2006, from http://www.preknow.org/documents/LeadershipReport_May2006.pdf

Lee, J. H., & Walsh, D. J. (2005). Early childhood program quality [Special issue]. *Early Education and Development, 16*(2).

Loeb, S., Fuller, B., Kagan, S. L., & Carrol, B. (2004). Child care in poor communities: Early learning effects of type of quality, and stability. *Child Development, 75*(1), 47–65. Retrieved June 28, 2006, from http://pace.berkeley.edu/Stanford_Child_Dev_Findings.pdf

Lynch, R. G. (2004). *Exceptional returns: Economic, fiscal, and social benefits of investment in early childhood development.* Washington, DC: Economic Policy Institute.

Mallory, B. L., & New, R. S. (1994). *Diversity and developmentally appropriate practice: Challenges for early childhood education.* New York: Teachers College Press.

Marcon, R. A. (1992). Differential effects of three preschool models on inner-city 4-year olds. *Early Childhood Research Quarterly, 7,* 517–530.

Marcon, R. A. (1999). Differential impact of preschool models on development and early learning of inner-city children: A three cohort study. *Developmental Psychology, 35,* 358–375.

Marcon, R. A. (2002). Moving up the grades: Relationship between preschool model and later school success. *Early Childhood Research and Practice, 4*(1). Retrieved June 12, 2002, from http://ecrp.uiuc.edu/v4n1/marcon.html

Marshall, N. L., Dennehy, J., Johnson-Staub, C., & Robeson, W. W. (2005). *Massachusetts capacity study research brief: Characteristics of the current early education and care workforce serving 3–5 year-olds.* Wellesley, MA: Wellesley Centers for Women.

Mathews, D., & McAfee, N. (1997). *Making choices together: The power of public deliberation.* Dayton, OH: Charles F. Kettering Foundation.

Mayo, A. J., & Nohria, N. (2005). Zeitgeist leadership. *Harvard Business Review, 83*(10), 45–60.

McDaniel, G. L., Issac, M. Y., Brooks, H. M., & Hatch, A. (2005). Confronting K–3 teaching challenges in an era of accountability. *Young Children, 60*(2), 22–26.

Michel, S. (1999). *Children's interests/mothers' rights.* New Haven, CT: Yale University Press.

Mitchell, A., & Modigliani, K. (1989). Young children in public schools: The "only ifs" reconsidered. *Young Children, 44*(6), 56–61.

Mitchell, A., Seligson, M., & Marx, F. (1987). *Early childhood programs and the public schools: Between promise and practice.* Dover, MA: Auburn House.

Monte, J. E., Xiang, Z., & Schweinhart, L. J. (2006). Preschool experience in 10 countries: Cognitive and language performance at age 7. *Early Childhood Research Quarterly, 21,* 313–331.

Morgan, G. (1998). *A hitchhiker's guide to the child care universe.* Washington, DC: National Association for Child Care Resource and Referral Agencies.

Morgan, G. (2006). *Is profession a noun?* Working paper.

Morgan, G., Azer, S., Costley, J., Genser, A., Goodman, I., Lombardi, J., et al. (1993). *Making a career of it: The state of the states report on career development in early care and education.* Boston: Center for Career Development in Early Care and Education at Wheelock College.

Morgan, G., & Costley, J. (2004). *Taking the temperature of career development.* Cambridge, MA: Lesley University Center for Children, Families and Public Policy.

Morgan, G., & Helburn, S. (2006, May/June). ECE meets economics. *Exchange,* No. 146, 10–14.

NAEYC early childhood program standards and accreditation criteria: The mark of quality in early childhood education. (2005). Washington, DC: National Association for the Education of Young Children.

National Association for the Education of Young Children. (2004, February 26). *Early education experts highlight concerns about new nationwide test of four-year olds in Head Start* [Press release]. Washington, DC: Author.

National Association for the Education of Young Children. (2005*). Code of ethical conduct and statement of commitment.* Washington, DC: Author. Retrieved March 10, 2006, from http://www.naeyc.org/about/positions/ethical_conduct.asp

National Association for the Education of Young Children. (n.d.). Membership options. Retrieved February 22, 2006, from http://www.naeyc.org/membership/options.asp

National Association of Elementary School Principals. (2005). *Leading early childhood learning communities: What principals should know and be able to do.* Alexandria, VA: Author.

National Association of Social Workers. (n.d.). Membership application. Retrieved February 22, 2006, from http://www.socialworkers.org/nasw/join/memberapplication.pdf

National Association of State Boards of Education. (2001, March). High-stakes testing of young children. *Policy Update, 9*(4).

National Institute for Early Childhood Professional Development. (1993). *Concept papers & National Institute for Professional Development background materials.* Washington, DC: National Association for the Education of Young Children.

National Research Council. (2001). *Eager to learn: Educating our preschoolers.* Committee on Early Childhood Pedagogy. B. T. Bowman, M. S. Donovan, & M. S. Burns (Eds.). Commission on Behavioral and Social Sciences and Education. Washington, DC: National Academy Press.

National Research Council and Institute of Medicine. (2000). *From neurons to neighborhoods: The science of early child development.* Committee on Integrating the Science of Early Childhood Development. J. P. Shonkoff & D. A. Phillips (Eds.). Board on Children, Youth, and Families, Commission on Behavioral and Social Sciences and Education. Washington, DC: National Academy Press.

Neugebauer, R. (2006). *For-profit care: Four decades of growth.* Retrieved February 19, 2006, from http://mail.ccie.com/go/eed/938

Oyemade, U. J., Washington, V., & Gullo, D. F. (1989, Winter). The relationship between Head Start parental involvement and the economic self-sufficiency of Head Start. *The Journal of Negro Education, 58*(1), 5–15.

Paulson, A. (2006, March 21). Illinois leads new push for universal preschool. *Christian Science Monitor.* Retrieved March 21, 2006, from http://www.csmonitor.com/2006/0321/p02s01-legn.html

Pizzo, P. (1983). Slouching toward Bethlehem: American federal policy perspectives on children and their families. In E. F. Zigler, S. L. Kagan, & E. Klugman (Eds.), *Children, families, and government: Perspectives on American social policy* (pp. 10–32). Cambridge: Cambridge University Press.

Pre-K education in the states. (2005, Spring). *Early Developments, 9*(1), 1, 6–9.

Public Agenda. (2000). *Necessary compromises: How parents, employers and children's advocates view child care today.* New York: Author.

Raver, C. C. (2002). *Emotions matter: Making the case for the role of young children's emotional development for early school readiness* (SRCD Social Policy Report, Vol. 16, No. 3). Ann Arbor, MI: Society for Research in Child Development.

Reynolds, A. J. (2000). *Success in early intervention: The Chicago child–parent centers.* Lincoln: University of Nebraska Press.

Rhode Island KIDS COUNT. (2005). *Getting ready: Findings from the national school readiness indicators initiative: A 17 state partnership.* Providence, RI: Author.

Rob Reiner takes leave from California Commission. (2006, March 8). *Education Week, 25*(2), 18.

Rodd, J. (1994). *Leadership in early childhood: The pathway to professionalism.* New York: Teachers College Press.

Rolnick, A., & Grunewald, R. (2003, October 17). *Early childhood development: Economic development with a high public return.* Presentation at the Economics of Early Childhood Development: Lessons for Economic Policy Conference, co-hosted by the Federal Reserve Bank of Minneapolis and the McKnight Foundation in cooperation with the University of Minnesota. Retrieved October 13, 2004, from http://minneapolisfed.org/pubs/fedgaz/03-03/earlychild.cfm

Saluja, G., Early, D. M., & Clifford, R. M. (2002, Spring). Demographic characteristics of early childhood teachers and structural elements of early care and education in the United States. *Early Childhood Research and Practice, 4*(1). Retrieved February 15, 2006, from http://ecrp.uiuc.edu/v4n1/saluja.html

Schein, E. H. (2004). *Organizational culture and leadership* (3rd ed.). San Francisco: Jossey Bass.

School readiness: Closing racial and ethnic gaps. [Special issue]. (2005). *The Future of Children, 15*(1).

Schumacher, K. I., & Lombardi, J. (2003). *Meeting great expectations: Integrating early education program standards in child care.* Washington, DC: Center for Law and Social Policy.

Schwartz, P. (2003). *Inevitable surprises: Thinking ahead in a time of turbulence.* New York: Gotham Books.

Schweinhart, L. J. (2004). *The High/Scope Perry Preschool study through age 40: Summary, conclusions, and frequently asked questions.* Ypsilanti, MI: High/Scope Educational Research Foundation.

Schweinhart, L. J., Barnes, H. V., & Weikart, D. P. (1993). *Significant benefits: The High/Scope Perry Preschool study through age 27.* Ypsilanti, MI: The High/Scope Press.

Schweinhart, L. J., & Weikart, L. J. (1997). The High/Scope Preschool curriculum comparison study through age 23. *Early Childhood Research Quarterly, 7,* 117–143.

Scott-Little, C., Kagan, S. L., & Frelow, V. S. (2003). *Standards for preschool children's learning and development: Who has the standards, how were they developed, and how were they used?* Greensboro, NC: Regional Educational Laboratory at SERVE.

Scott-Little, C., Kagan, S. L., & Frelow, V. S. (2006). Conceptualization of readiness and the content of early learning standards: The intersection of policy and research? *Early Childhood Research Quarterly, 21,* 153–173.

Senge, P. M. (1990). *The fifth discipline: The art and practice of the learning organization.* New York: Doubleday.

Senge, P. (1999). The leadership of profound change. In Senge, P., Kleiner, A., Roberts, C., Ross, R., Roth, G., & Smith, B. (Eds.), *The dance of change: The challenges of sustaining momentum in learning organizations* (pp. 10–21). New York: Doubleday.

Senge, P. M., & Kaufer, K. H. (n.d.). *Communities of leaders or no leadership at all.* Retrieved October 10, 2005, from http://www.dialogonleadership.org/SengeKauefer.pdf

Senge, P., Kleiner, A., Roberts, C., Ross, R., Roth, G., & Smith, B. (1999). *The dance of change: The challenges of sustaining momentum in learning organizations.* New York: Doubleday.

Set for success: Building a strong foundation for school readiness based on the social-emotional development of young children. (2002). Kansas City, MO: Ewing Marion Kauffman Foundation.

Shore, R. (1997). *Rethinking the brain: New insights into early development.* New York: Families and Work Institute.

Slaughter, D. T., Washington, V., Oyemade, U. J., & Lindsey, R. W. (1988, Summer). *Head Start: A backward and forward look* (Vol. III, No. 2). Washington, D.C.: Society for Research in Child Development.

Smith, M. M. (1987). NAEYC at 60: Visions for the year 2000. *Young Children, 42*(3), 33–39.

Snyder, A. (1972). *Dauntless women in childhood education: 1856–1931.* Washington, DC: Association for Childhood Education International.

Steinberg, J. (2002, December 4). For Head Start children, their turn at testing [Education column]. *New York Times,* p. 10.

Stepping up together: Financing early care and education in the 21st century. (1999). *Proceedings for making it economically viable: Financing early care and education* (Vol. 2). Kansas City, MO: Ewing Marion Kauffman Foundation.

Swadener, B. B., & Kessler, S. (Eds.). (1991). Reconceptualizing early childhood education [Special issue]. *Early Education and Development, 2*(2).

Sykes, G. (1987). Reckoning with the spectre. *Education Researcher, 16*(4), 19–21.

Takanishi, R. (2004). *Grantmakers for Children, Youth and Families (GCYF) presented Dr. Takanishi with the 2004 Fred Rogers Leadership Award.* Retrieved September 3, 2005, from http://www.fcd-us.org/news/RTSpeech.html

Talan, T. N., & Bloom, P. J. (2004). *Program administration scale.* New York: Teachers College Press.

Tobin, J. J. (1992). Early childhood education and the public schools: Obstacles to reconstructing a relationship. *Early Education and Development, 3*(2), 196–200.

U.S. Department of Health and Human Services, Administration for Children and Families, Office of Head Start. (n.d.). *Head Start program performance standards and other regulations.* Retrieved March 20, 2006, from http://www.acf.hhs.gov/programs/hsb/performance/index.htm

U.S. General Accounting Office. (1998, June*). Head Start: Challenges in monitoring program quality and demonstrating results.* Washington, DC: Author.

Washington, V. (2005). Sharing leadership: A case study of diversity in our profession. *Young Children, 60*(1), 23–31.

Washington, V., & Andrews, J. D. (Eds.). (1998). *Children of 2010.* Washington, DC: National Association for the Education of Young Children.

Washington, V., Ferris, M., Hughes, M., Scott-Chandler, S., Luk, W., & Bates, T. (2006). Family support: An essential component for effective preschool programs. *Perspectives, 2*, 31–36.

Washington, V., Marshall, N., Robinson, C., Modigliani, K., & Rosa, M. (2006, February 14). *Keeping the promise: A study of the Massachusetts child care voucher system.* Boston: Bessie Tartt Wilson Children's Foundation.

Washington, V., & Oyemade, U. J. (1995). *Project Head Start: Models, strategies and issues for the twenty-first century.* New York: Garland.

What's in a name? Practitioners' preference about terminology. (2001, Summer). In *Research Notes.* Wheeling, IL: McCormick Tribune Center for Early Childhood Leadership.

Wheatley, M. J. (1992). *Leadership and the new science: Learning about organization from an orderly universe.* San Francisco: Berrett-Koehler.

Whitebook, M. (2002). *Working for worthy wages: The child care compensation movement 1970–2001.* Berkeley, CA: Institute of Industrial Relations, Center for the Study of Child Care Employment.

Whitebook, M. (2003). *Early education quality: Higher teacher qualifications for better work environments—A review of the literature.* Berkeley, CA: Institute of Industrial Relations, Center for the Study of Child Care Employment.

Whitebook, M., & Phillips, D. (1999). *Child care employment: Implications for women's self sufficiency and for child development* (Working paper series). New York: Foundation for Child Development.

Whitebook, M., Sakai, L., Gerber, E., & Howes, C. (2001). *Then and now: Changes in child care staffing 1994–2000.* Washington, DC: Center for the Child Care Workforce.

Your child birth to three [Special edition]. (2000, Fall/Winter). *Newsweek.*

Your child from birth to three [Special edition]. (1997, Spring/Summer). *Newsweek.*

Zander, R. S., & Zander, B. (2000). *The art of possibility.* Boston: Harvard Business School Press.

Zigler, E., & Muenchow, S. (1992). *Head Start: The inside story of America's most successful educational experiment.* New York: Basic Books.

About the Authors

With over 50 years of combined experience, Stacie Goffin and Valora Washington are recognized authorities in early care and education. Each has been involved in leading significant change initiatives. Spanning higher education; local, state, and federal government; organizational development; research; and advocacy, their efforts have resulted in change for both policy and practice.

Stacie G. Goffin designs, facilitates, and implements strategic and field-building initiatives. Well known for her organizational capacity, analytical insights, and big-picture thinking, she directs major field-wide initiatives, such as Ohio's School Readiness Solutions Group and NAEYC's 5-year project to reinvent its nationally recognized early childhood program accreditation system. She led the founding—and served as founding chair—of the Early Childhood Funders Collaborative, the West Virginia Network for Young Children, and Kansas City's Metropolitan Council on Early Learning. A former senior program officer at the Ewing Marion Kauffman Foundation, she began her career as a preschool and primary grade teacher of children with special needs. She also has taught extensively at the undergraduate and graduate levels. A member of numerous ogranization and editorial boards, she has authored or edited more than 50 publications, including both editions of *Curriculum Models and Early Childhood Education: Appraising the Relationship* and *Whither Early Childhood Care and Education in the Next Century?* in the centennial volume of the National Society for the Study of Education.

Valora Washington directs several leadership programs for practitioners, including the Schott Fellowship in Early Care and Education and the Principals Fellowship for elementary school principals with prekindergarten programs—both of which offer new models for leadership development. She also has co-created several institutions, such as Michigan's Children, a statewide advocacy group, and the Early Childhood Funders Collaborative. Frequently tapped for senior-level service, she has been Co-Chair of the Massachusetts School Readiness Commission, Board Chair for Voices for America's Children, Secretary of NAEYC, chair of the Black Caucus of the Society for Research in Child Development, and Co-Chair of the National Head Start Association Commission on 2010. She currently serves as a trustee of the Boston Children's Museum and Wheelock College. A former Vice-President of the Kellogg Foundation, she is a co-author or co-editor of over 50 publications, including *Children of 2010* and *Keeping the Promise: A Study of the Massachusetts Child Care Voucher System*. She was educated at both Indiana and Michigan State Universities and holds honorary doctorate degrees from both Bennett College and the Meadville Lombard Theological School. She is a Certified Association Executive with the American Society of Association Executives.

Index